Copyright © 2015 by Dr. T.L. Osborn
Published by 410-HOPE Publishing

Books published by 410-HOPE Publishing are available at special discount for bulk purchases in the United States for corporations, institutes, and other organizations. For more information, please contact me at thehiphoplectures@gmail.com

Text set in 13.5-point Arial Narrow
Includes bibliographical references and Index

A CIP catalog record for this book is available from the Library of Congress.

ISBN: 10: 0986104108
ISBN: 13: 978-0-9861041-0-7 (Printed Version)

Acknowledgements

This book is dedicated to a couple of people starting with Patricia (Mom aka "Love" aka Ma' Pat), Kimberly (Big Little Sister aka "Faith" aka Keezy), and DeLena (Linka aka Bestie aka Right-hand).

This book is dedicated to my family and those who became my family, which includes Grandma (aka Mattie), Grandpa, Ms. Twiggy, Erin, Tiffany, Nyasha (aka Nynia), Ms. Sonya, Ms. Nancy, Ms. Sandra, Kamila, Swapna, Aunt Holly, Aunt Shirley, Uncle Ricky, Dr. Roseboro, Tahmar, and anyone with "a dollar and a dream."

This book is dedicated to my co-workers and students from Dance 147 (aka Hip Hop History Lecture Class), since 2006.

Last, but not least this book is dedicated to GOD!

The Hip Hop Lectures

(Volume 1)

By:

Dr. T.L. Osborne

Table of Contents

Introduction: Why Am I Writing This Book?

Introduction: Why Am I Writing This Book?

There are many aspects of Hip Hop culture that exceeds beyond just the beat, a dance, or a catchy hook. *The Hip Hop Lectures (Volume 1)* is a book that was created to make a connection between the past and the present, as it relates to Hip Hop culture. Hip Hop culture has been able to accomplish so much in such a very short period of time, most of which includes the bridging of generational and racial gaps locally and internationally. The hope; however, is that the culture continues to grow and evolve to a point where decades and centuries later, people will still be talking about some of the pioneers and innovators of such a wonderful musically inspired movement. *The Hip Hop Lectures (Volume 1)* is not the know-it-all of the Hip Hop culture or any culture, but an honest attempt to provide insight about how the past affects the present and future. *The Hip Hop Lectures (Volume 1)* is inspired by actual lectures used to teach anyone who has an interest in Hip Hop culture, beyond just music.

Discussing the connections between Hip Hop culture and history is significant. The fact that Hip Hop culture's history derives from the continent of Africa and currently expands throughout the world is nothing shorter than amazing. Each topic mentioned in this book could have its own volume of work; however, the content expressed is condensed in a way to provide the reader with basic historical information and encourage personal reflection and research. Understanding the historical connection between Hip Hop and history, allows one to realize how the youth of an enslaved culture have managed to create a world-wide multi-billionaire phenomenon known as Hip Hop culture. For anyone to come from "Nothing into something" is inspirational. After reading this book, my sincerest hope is that anyone who reads this book will be able to appreciate Hip Hop culture and see the culture's value on an educational level; in

spite of the good, bad, and indifferent sides of the culture.

Thank you for picking this book to read. I "HOPE" you enjoy

reading my life's passion.

Chapter 1
African Music History: The Originators

Historically, Hip Hop culture is known to have started in

New York; during the early 1970s. However, controversy

surrounds which specific area in New York created the cultural

phenomenon, called Hip Hop. The history concerning which

part of New York created this influential and multi-billion dollar

movement is documented in 1985. The battle rap included

rappers from Queensbridge (MC Shan & The Juice Crew)

versus rappers from the South Bronx (KRS-One & Boogie Down

Productions). Even though, New York, is noted as the

birthplace for Hip Hop culture, Hip Hop's roots were developed

before one city or state declared ownership of the cultures'

creation. Hip Hop's founding dj's, breakdancers, and mc's all

have roots that trace back to Africa.

No one knows who specifically created the first musical

rendition in history; however, the impact of African drumming and dancing is essential to Hip Hop culture's birth. Africa has a rich history rooted in dance, music, and song. Typically, when discussing African cultural history, the authors who document and reveal the historical perspective of Africans are normally written by non-Africans (specifically Anglo-Saxons and Europeans). Possible reasons for *why* Anglo-Saxon and European narratives were primary sources for African history, in America, could be based on the assumptions that:

1) African tribes limited cultural traditions and history to their tribes only. Therefore, Anglo-Saxon and European narratives of understanding African culture and history becomes essential.
2) Most Africans (before slavery) did not read, write, or have resources to publishing African history locally or abroad. Therefore, Anglo-Saxon and European narratives of understanding African culture and history becomes essential.

3) Because most African tribes preferred to tell their history orally, the written history and experiences of Africans were not considered as pertinent. Therefore, Anglo-Saxon and European narratives detailing African culture and history becomes essential.

4) African culture and history was loss, during the slave trade. Therefore, Anglo-Saxon and European narratives of understanding African culture and history becomes essential.

5) Once Africans were enslaved in America, the slave codes prevented slaves from reading and writing. As a result, no first-hand accounts during and immediately after slavery were written. Therefore, Anglo-Saxon and European narratives of understanding African culture and history becomes essential.

Anglo-Saxons and European narratives often focused on selective experiences of Africans. For example, Anglo-Saxon and European narratives about Africans and tribal rituals often limited the intellectual abilities of Africans, but highlighted

3

Africans natural affinity for physical activities such as drumming and dancing. Narratives would also discuss the frequency by which Africans danced. Because African history and culture were primarily part of an oral tradition, when Anglo-Saxon and European narratives were written, the language barrier between the cultures could have potentially rendered historical discrepancies and inconsistencies surrounding some of the cultural practices, traditions, and ways concerning African life. Also, the language barrier, most likely caused aspects of the African experience to be misinterpreted and some African concepts to be taken out of context.

Despite the limited narratives from Africans before, during, or directly after slavery, one particular African perspective was documented. Olaudah Equiano (1745-1797); also known as Gustavus Vassa, managed to document and publish his first-hand experiences, after being part of the West Indies slave trade and transitioning to American states like Virginia and Georgia

(Equiano, 2005). Equiano's historic narrative and selective

comments about his experiences and those of African people,

during and after slavery, serves as validation for first-hand

experiences. Equiano, in his self-published narrative, written in

1789, asserted, "We [Africans] are almost a nation of dancers,

musicians, and poets" (Equiano, 2005). Equiano's assertion

about Africa being a nation of dancers, musicians, and poets, is

concept that is quoted often, in other Anglo-Saxon and European

narratives. Unfortunately, this quote has dualistic intention. The

quote can be perceived as being both complimentary as well as

potentially damaging for Africans and eventually African

Americans. An old adage says, "First impressions last a lifetime."

Equiano's impression on African history, from a first-hand account

(as an African) is intriguing. The complimentary side of Equiano's

assertion is that Africans appear to have a natural affinity towards dancing, music, and poetry. However, the potentially damaging

part of his assertion is that Africans greatness may only be limited

to dancing, music, and poetry.

The limitations of Equiano's statement can be interpreted

in different ways, just as a rapper's lyrics can be interpreted.

However, the coincidence of Equiano's wording may not be as

easy to ignore; especially given the potential options for success

for African Americans, in America. Equiano's, 1789, summation-

describing Africa as a nation of dancers, musicians, and poets

has prophetic relevance to how current success can be achieved.

For example, the popular and influential 1990's rapper, Notorious

B.I.G., in the song, *Things Done Changed (1994),* says:

> If I wasn't in the rap game/
> I'd probably have a key knee deep in the crack game/
> Because the streets is a short stop/
> Either you're slingin' crack rock or you got a wicked jump
> shot/

Notorious B.I.G., in these rap lyrics, presents an alternative and

evolved version of Equiano's description of African people.

Instead of being a nation of dancers, musicians, and poets,

Notorious' lyrics claim that "the nation" is now a nation of rappers

(entertainers), drug dealers, and athletes. Is this perception by

Notorious B.I.G. from the 1990's currently relative, negative,

positive, or truthful? Or, are Notorious' lyrics irrelevant, because

the beat, in the song, makes your head rock back-and-forth;

overshadowing one's ability to even process the words?

Equiano most likely did not intend on limiting his own

African culture to three categorizations; however, his statements

created the foundation for stereotypes surrounding current

Africans and future African Americans. In other words, Equiano's

first-hand account of Africans validates all of the second-hand

accounts about Africans (African Americans) that some

Eurocentric people have about the African people then and

current notions about African Americans. One particular stereotype that would become prominent within and outside of the African community is that people of African descent; specifically African Americans, have a natural proclivity for entertainment and not education. The people of Africa were much more than entertainment for travelers visiting Africa.

When Equiano affirms the thoughts of Eurocentric people, by stating that Africa is a nation of dancers, musicians, and poets this stereotype seems more than just an outsider's (Eurocentric) perception of African peoples' limitations, but also appears to be a premonition for how some Africans may perceive their cultural worth. Therefore, when visitors come to Africa, they expected to see Africans entertain them, because that is what Eurocentric narratives and the African, Equiano, says happens. Do you see the irony in this scenario? Words can transcend moments and time in un-imaginable ways. Equiano often shared his personal thoughts and experiences. However, his choice of words; whether intentional or un-intentional, describing Africans as a nation of dancers, musicians, and poets continues to have a lasting impression and impact on future generations; especially the Hip Hop culture.

African Dancers (Original Breakdancers)

If the drummer (and eventually the Dj) is considered the backbone of African culture and Hip Hop music, then the dancers serve as muses for the drummer. In African culture, traditional tribal dances could last for days at a time, depending on the purpose of the ceremony or ritual. Traditional African dancers dance without hesitation and are not easily persuaded to dance on a singular beat. In fact, African dancers are polyrhythmic dancers, which means they dance on multiple beats. Drummers, in Africa, have an innate ability to play beats, which allows dancers to express their emotions freely without having to worry about being on a specific beat. The dancers' movements can inspire the drummers' beats, just as the drummers' beats can inspire the dancers' movements. Dancing on any beat (upbeat or downbeat) is considered a gift in African culture, because just as beats vary in sound and tempo, so does one's emotions and experiences. African dancing is *not* meant to be stylish or cool, but created to encourage everyone to dance freely without restrictions or inhibitions.

To encourage everyone to dance freely, Africans typically organize drumming and dancing events from a hierarchical perspective. In African culture, dancing is organized based on a specific hierarchy: 1) married men 2) married women 3) young men and 4) young maidens (Equiano, 2005). The hierarchy, in African culture, allows each group to adequately express themselves, while dualistically identifying cultural status, preserving order, and establishing unity within the culture.

Outside the celebratory events that involve everyone, African culture dancing is based on gender, age, and status. The married men often danced for specific purposes, in African culture (Welsh, 2004). War, hunting, and agriculture are key events that evoke married men to dance (Gates and Appiah, 1999). Married women often danced for specific purposes, which included weddings, funerals, baby tooth loss, births, pregnancies, and fertility (Gates and Appiah, 1999). Young men often danced for hunting and agriculture, as well, but often is celebrated during coming of age ceremonies (Gates and Appiah, 1999). The young maidens danced for weddings, funerals, baby tooth loss, births, and menstruation (Gates and Appiah, 1999). The drummer and dancer(s) are intertwined and the multiple variation of beats allow for non-stop dancing.

Each group (married men, married women, young men, and young maidens) is allowed the freedom of expression individually, while still maintaining a collective unity. Because each group gets an opportunity to dance, no one person or group feels limited in their expressions or experiences. Oftentimes when married men dance, the dances include weapons and aggressive behavior and mannerisms. Any of the emotions expressed by men, during African dancing events, could be harmful to women, because women have differing experiences, behaviors, and mannerisms than men. Therefore, there is no need to have the two groups (females and males) dance together and inhibit one another's expression of emotions. Additionally, separating the groups (females and males), when dancing, can preserve one's marital and virginal status. Married males, in the tribe, should not be dancing with the young maidens (single women). If married men began to dance with young maidens the tribal community would no longer be unified, but become disjointed; resulting in continual arguments and endless infidelity issues.

Traditional African dancing still has purpose and relevancy today. Although men and women, in American culture do not dance in separate groups or hierarchies, the desire to express one's self freely in dance is universal. When discussing how to look cool or un-cool, when dancing, people often refer to dancing as being "on beat" or "off beat." Dancing "off-beat," typically, includes having a fast and non-rhythmic tempo, while dancing "on-beat" is normally includes having a slow and rhythmic tempo. Dancing "off-beat" is synonymous with moving without thinking or feeling and "on-beat" dancing is synonymous with thinking and waiting to feel the beat. In other words, stereotypical lenses would say that all people of European descent naturally dance "off-beat" because as soon as the music comes on (the 1, 3, 5, 7), they dance. However, stereotypical lenses would also say that all people of African descent *naturally* dance "on-beat" because they wait to feel (the 2, 4, 6, and 8) the music before just dancing.

Discussions about the natural ability to dance "on-beat" versus "off-beat," continues to promote stereotypes. Stereotypes, such as, "All African American people have natural rhythm." This stereotype is untrue, but is often promoted in society and culturally as being a definitive truth. For example, the television show, *The Fresh Prince of Bel Air*, which premiered on September 10, 1990, starring Will Smith and Alfonso Ribeiro (who played Will Smith's cousin Carlton) revealed that all African American people *do not* have natural rhythm. In just a few episodes, television viewers quickly learned that Will and his cousin Carlton; although both African American lived two separate lives and had different experiences (TvGuide Online, 2014). Will was urban and Carlton was suburban. Will danced "on-beat" and Carlton "off-beat," despite both being African Americans. In fact,

Carlton, danced "off-beat" (on the 1, 3, 5, 7) frequently and

proudly often to Tom Jones 1965 song, *It's Not Unusual.*

Carlton's love for Tom Jones' song destroys any notion or

stereotype that says all black people or people of African descent

have a natural ability to dance "on beat." Carlton's excitement

and dance was unusual, if you are looking at him through

stereotypical lenses. However, if looking from historical lenses of

relevancy to African cultural music, one immediately realizes that

dancing is not about being "on-beat" or "off-beat," but inspiring

one to be free. Even though, *The Fresh Prince of Bel Air* was a

television show, the story line of Carlton's dancing, as an African

American, is realistic, because dancing is not something that is

relegated to timed steps or looking cool; especially in African

culture.

Hip Hop culture, however, may publically emphasize and

promote the idea of dancing "on-beat" (the 2, 4, 6, 8 beat aka the downbeat/cool beat); but ironically, the 1, 3, 5, and 7 (aka the upbeat/off-beat) beats are prevalent in certain Hip Hop dances, such as *Krumping*. *Krumping* was popularized around the mid-1990s and includes dance movements that are similar to African male tribal dances, which includes dancing on multiple beats and tempos. Another similar African tradition that is currently practiced by people (unknowingly) who dance on the "on-beat or off-beat," is the dance formation. Have you ever noticed how at dance or party venues, when people begin to express themselves (in dance, song, or performance) the crowd immediately disperses into a circle to watch the person. As a society of "on-beat and off-beat" dancing people, we naturally move into a circled position of observation and support enthusiastically. Notice that those watching the dancer(s), do not form a triangle, square, a rectangle, or have someone directing the crowd on how to surround the dancer(s) to watch the performance. People naturally form a perfectly structured circle to watch people dance, which is the same dance formation that Africans used called, the ring circle.

The Drummers (The Original Dj's)

There are additional drums and instruments used in African culture, such as the bougarabou, the tama talking drum, ngoma drums, water drums, xylophones, flutes, and bells (Blanc, 1997). However, in African culture, the drum is: sacred, represents the "heartbeat" of the African people, named accordingly based on its purpose. For example, the Djembe drum is used to gather everyone; Dje=gather and BE=everyone (Blanc, 1997). Drums, like the Djembe are purposefully named; however, emphasis is also placed on what makes the drum. In African culture, the drum is comprised of three important elements: the animal skin, the wood, and the spirit of the drummer (Blanc, 1997). The three elements of the drum reveal how the drummer and the drum are one-in-the-same. This also explains why some

drummers may sound different from other drummers when

playing; even if the drummers are playing the same drum the

same way. The connection between the drummer and the drum

is important to know because writing and reading came late to

certain parts of Africa, which means that music (specifically

drumbeats) was an important and main form of communication.

African drummers have an uncanny ability to create beats that

can simultaneously communicate messages and evoke

responses spoken and unspoken. This communication shared

between a drummer and the audience is similar to the call and

response technique that is used when someone is speaking or

singing and seeking a response from the crowd. For instance,

have you ever noticed when you hear an instrumental (beats) to a

song, you have a natural ability to decipher the mood of that song,

before you hear the lyrics? The instrumental (beats) dictates the

18

purpose and intention of a song before words or lyrics are added to the beats. In addition, the drummers' beats are created for various reasons and inspired by varying experiences; proving that beats are used for more than just celebratory events and dancing, in African culture. Depending on the tribe, certain beats were used for more than just entertainment or expression purposes. Certain beats when played served as a communicative tool and strategy to warn the community about arriving visitors or signal that enemies approaching.

When entertaining and creating beats for dancers, African drummers dictate the mood of dancers, by changing the pace of a beat and using variations of sound (polyphonic). Typically, in African culture when music is played, the drummers and dancers are often aligned in a circle; specifically a ring circle. The ring circle is significant because the circle represents a sense of unity and community. Within the ring circle, there is always a minimum of two drummers. Having a minimum of two drummers allows each drummer the opportunity to incorporate multiple rhythms (polyrhythms) that can be played endlessly. Drummers typically play two standard beats: 1) upbeats and 2) downbeats. Discussing upbeats and downbeats can be difficult to understand, depending on how educators, musicians, and dancers describe the beats. Even though both beats (the up and down) are considered part of the 8-count, the upbeat is described as 1, 3, 5, and 7 and the downbeat as 2, 4, 6, and 8. Interestingly, the two beats are not permanently defined and are interchangeably. Additionally, some music theorists describe the idea of "upbeat and downbeat" as a person standing up and lifting his or her foot up in the air. The upward lift of the foot would be considered the upbeat. Then every time the same person's foot goes back down towards the ground that would be the downbeat (the downward motion of the foot).

Despite the downbeat being associated with rhythm, style, and coolness; in Hip Hop and popular culture, those who practice traditional African cultural dances do not preference one beat (upbeat or downbeat) over another. In fact, music in African culture is often used to encourage people to express themselves freely without limitations and with the spirit of inclusiveness and respect regarding one's dance styles. Dancing, in African culture, focuses on expressing one's self without being inhibited by the rhythm, style of music, or who is watching. In African culture, people are free to dance and express themselves by dancing on any beat; the downbeat, upbeat, or both beats. Because both beats matter and are equally valuable is an essential aspect of African music. Being aware that music, in African culture, is primarily used for self-expression removes the pressure of trying to look cool or be "on beat," while dancing and instead encourages dancing without judgement or regret. In the end, the motto is simple: "The beat that one likes is the beat that one should dance on without concern."

In African culture, the drummer can create the mood, pace, and influence the style of dance. In Hip Hop culture, the Dj operates in the same manner as the African drummers operate in while in the ring circle. Traditional Hip Hop Dj's often functioned using a turntable, which played a minimum of two albums/songs at a time. Traditional Dj's often pieced together music by: 1) using turntables, 2) incorporating two different songs from two different albums, while simultaneously blending and mixing those sounds, and 3) connecting those two distinct songs to create one massive and continuous beat, which would eventually become known as the breakbeat. The breakbeat is considered the most popular part of an album. Just like African drummers go back-and-forth between drumbeats, traditional Dj's (using turntables) go back-and-forth between breakbeats allowing the audience to enjoy their favorite parts of songs non-stop. The same level of enjoyment that dj's provide encourages people to keep dancing and expressing one's self all night long; similar to African drummers. The excitement and non-stop dancing is similar to the African drum and dancing. The African drummers became Hip Hop Dj's, which is considered the backbone of Hip Hop culture. Interestingly enough, many of the Hip Hop Dj's that helped build the dj'ing culture of Hip Hop, have evolved beyond the turntables and have become music producers.

The Griots (Original Mc's)

Most cultures have someone who often serves as a story-teller or historian for the community. In African culture, this individual is called the griot. The griot was an important part of African culture and was respected like a king and treated like royalty. The griot is considered a master and is invaluable to African culture. Many people, including Alex Haley (writer and producer of the series entitled *Roots*) asserts, "When a griot dies, it is as if a library has burned to the ground" (Chang and Terry, 2007, p.13). The griot was a position of esteem. Griots memorize the history and traditions of their tribes and then transpose that history into music by identifying all that is relevant, important, and inspiring. Griots would often share the history of the tribe's origins and victories in war to entertain, celebrate, and motivate the tribal leaders, warriors, and members of the community. The griot often told stories (in the ring circles, just like the drummers) and would improvise realistic and fictional stories about daily occurrences and life-lessons. The call and response technique was often used by griots to engage and interact with members of the audience.

Positions of esteem, in African culture are male dominated. Despite the depth of knowledge, wisdom, talent, and reverence associated with the griot, in African culture, the griots' position is limited only to men and male apprentices. Gender roles exists

throughout history and often dictate the roles and responsibilities

of women and men. Therefore, knowing that drumming and

becoming a griot were both male specific roles, one should not be

surprised to see why women throughout history; specifically

female rappers, struggle to become equal to their male peers.

Despite the gender roles, the similarities between the griots and

rap mc's are identical. For example:

- Griots often told stories about their tribes/tribesmen, while
  mc's/rappers tell stories about their hoods or environment.
- Griots would often formed circles when sharing stories and
  playing music, while rappers often form cyphers (rap
  circles where mc's/rappers take turns rapping).
- Griots also improvised (came up with stories on the spot),
  when around live audiences, while rappers/mc's often
  free-style (come up with rap lyrics on the spot).
- Griots often told realistic and fictional stories of tribal life
  and experiences to invigorate, motivate, and share to

audiences, while mc's/ rappers typically rap about true and false stories.

The griots legacy is intertwined within the history that he knows and shares with the community. Each of these aspects of African culture (drumming, dancing, story-telling) are all foundational to Hip Hop's culture. Music in African culture was a 24/7 event. In other words, music in African culture was like having your own musical soundtrack following you wherever you go; before mp3 players were created. Because Africa is vast and includes various regions, the music of Africa is an assortment of dance styles and beats, which is why some of the main aspects of African culture could be preserved and practiced while in America.

Chapter 2
The Party is Over: A New Journey Without Beats & Freedom

The early perceptions of African tribesmen were that these outsiders (Anglo-Saxon and European visitors) were unassuming and non-threatening. Most of the outsiders (Anglo-Saxon and European visitors) initially came in peace without incident, conducted research for educational purposes, and in some cases offered an opportunity for more Africans to become Christian. African culture history and early writings included information about various tribes and African traditions. History and writings also explained how quintessential music was for the people and how music was the center of each tribal visit, conversation, celebration, and event. As mentioned in the previous chapter, most of the historic information concerning Africans revealed that Africans enjoyed music and entertaining primarily. Unfortunately, there was rarely a discussion about the deeper connection with the music and how the music represented their lifeline and intertwined with the spirit of Africans. Music, in African culture, is the African's sole basis for living and the beat of the drum, which is symbolic to the heartbeat, serves as the lifeline for the African culture collectively and the individual.

African music is infused with an array of culturally diverse elements. From the polyrhythmic drumbeats that incorporate the African people's heartbeats and experiences to the need to express one's self freely through dance has always been foundational to understanding the essence of the culture. Unfortunately, the freedom of expression, the heartfelt connections with the beat, and experiences that Africans valued, in Africa, would never be the same, once slave trading began. The transition from Africa to America (The Middle Passage Voyage) potentially threatened the existence of a people, sought to eradicate the power of music, and destroy the spirit of Africans.

Before you continue to read Chapter 2, please take a moment and reflect on the idea of slavery in relation to America and Africans, as well as how Africans became slaves and arrived in America. If you do not know about slavery in America or cannot recall what occurred, take a moment and conduct your own brief research (using any reputable search engine). What you will immediately notice is the how many ways that Africans were purchased, captured, and forced into slavery in America. Secondly, you will notice how many unimaginably things happened to these Africans, before even becoming slaves in America. In other words, the journey to enslavement in America was traumatic, horrendous, and gruesome.

Imagine moments when Africans could spend hours reflecting on the simplest things in life, which created happiness and unity. African culture embraces every aspect of life and every, no matter how big or small the experiences. African tribes would celebrate a baby losing a tooth by having people dance for hours or days. Africans would dance to celebrate rain falling from the sky, because the rain provided water and nourishment to the soil to help crops grow successfully. Africans often sung and danced to show praise for safety, life, and victory from sons, husbands, and fathers returning home from a hunting expedition or war. Africans celebrated of life-and-death because life and death were both joyous occasions. Life was always a blessing, because of the opportunity to fulfill one's purpose. However, death was also worthy of celebration because one's death was an opportunity to celebrate everything that a person accomplished while living. Death was a culmination of someone's life and provided moments for reflecting gratefulness of that person's life today, tomorrow, and eternally. Death also was an opportunity to gain another angel to protect and overlook you, while you are still living.

The connection between Africans and cultural traditions such as drumming, dancing, and music were provides a lot of understanding. The social, physical, psychological, and emotional purposes of these traditions were monumental to the African people. The loss of these cultural traditions sheds light on how impactful the transition of Africans to America was and how much history was lost through captivity. In other words, the Africans not only lost their physical freedom but the freedom to engage in cultural traditions, during the slave trade voyage and upon their arrival in America as slaves. The reality that Africans were forced to transition from a life of freedom and enjoyment to a life of constant torment, degradation, control, and fear is unimaginable. Being in a constant mindset that: recycles an array of emotions, struggles to imagine freedom, and reflects only memories of happiness in hindsight with no hope insight is devastating. The newly expressed emotions of these Africans, who are now slaves, reflect a life that no longer exists and a life that will never be the same. Going from knowing and experiencing freedom to being forced to forget everything you know and love and being permanently bound is a tormenting state to live in. This new enslaved life was literally like dying a thousand deaths daily after already living a full and enjoyable life. Life, the way Africans knew life to be, no longer exists. The hope of an entire culture struggles to remain in a minuscule part each Africans spirit that arrived in America.

Discussing when, why, and how Africans arrived in America, many questions could arise. For instance, if someone were to ask you, how did Africans end up enslaved in America, what would you say? Would you begin to share everything you learned in school from teachers, saw in movies, heard on the radio, or read in various books? Would you believe everything or be leery about what you were told, what you read, or what you have seen? Knowing the details of how Africans arrived in America is an important part of American history. However, understanding the impact of Africans' arrival to America as slaves provides cultural significance to the Africans experiences historically, presently, and futuristically.

History records the first Africans arrival, in Jamestown, Virginia, in 1619 (Davis, 1998). However, there are questions about whether the Africans were indentured servants (temporary status) or slaves (permanent status). Also, the status of the Africans were questionable, because some historical documents reveal that some Africans had been living and working in America willingly; before slaves arrived in 1619. In other words, if some Africans were already living and working in America, how did they get here? The response to this question may vary, because the enslavement was designed strategically for permanent enslavement of Africans not just a randomly or temporarily executed plan.

Admitting that slavery was strategically brilliant creates contention because within this statement is an acknowledgment that something so horrendous was done so magnificently. The process of capturing and enslaving Africans included an assortment of techniques that have had an undeniable mark on American history and have impacted generations of people. Contrary to what one may think, Africans were not simply gathered in a field, chained, forced to march to a seashore, and then led to the bottom of a ship. In fact, because of the strategic nature of slavery, one could potentially say enslaving Africans included multiple phases. For example, an 8-step phase, which *probably* included:

A period of observation

To truly capture one's enemy effectively, a period of studying the enemy is essential. Observation can come from up-close. For example, when outsiders, scholars, and potential slave traders would visit Africa and African tribes first-hand, outsiders/visitors would document their experiences based on observing the daily occurrences of a tribe. The documenting of their experiences in the moment or in retrospect often included revealing: what was seen, how the men, women, and children interacted, how often music is played, the importance of cultural traditions and hierarchies, specific uses for the drum, and strengths and weaknesses within the culture. However, some of the observation can occur from afar. For example, potential slave traders would have access to these same documented writings written from outsiders, visitors, and scholars perspectives. After reviewing some of the information, these same slave traders could gather the first-hand information and study the inner workings of Africans, their culture, their war practices, and other vital information that would become detrimental to the Africans.

A period of deceitful bonding

The best approach to gaining trust is to create a pseudo bond. Developing positive relationships and interactions between slave traders and Africans were an essential part of the process, when it came to capturing and enslaving Africans. Because some Africans became familiar with some of these visitors and outsiders the lines of communication increased over time. In addition, a sense of openness and familiarity towards outside visitors, missionaries, and travelers created a belief among many Africans that the relationships being developed were sincere and mutually treasured. Because the bond being developed was appearing to grow stronger with each interaction, many Africans were initially unaware of any ill-will or deceit from these visitors who often times appeared to be in awe and amazement of the Africans and their cultural traditions. Therefore, when a constant barrage of gifts and offerings were given by the outsiders/visitors with every visit to the Africans and their tribal leaders a bond was established. Eventually all-access to tribal kings, leaders, traditions, insights, and practices were garnered.

A period of embracement

Embracing one's culture can create a feeling of unity and respect. Outsiders, scholars, and potential slave traders would engage the African tribes and show signs of respect for the tribe's uniqueness and value. Potential acts of embracement would even include participating in sacred events, ring dances, the sharing of religious teachings, teaching of dialect, and sharing of cultural knowledge, history, and insights. Having direct access with tribal leaders and kings revealed immense comfortability between Africans and travelers, which allowed for tribal secrecies, philosophies, communication practices, and in some cases war strategies to be compromised.

A period of gift-giving and trades

Gift-giving is a great technique and often a sign of thoughtfulness and appreciation. Outsiders, scholars, and potential slave traders would visit various tribes and offer thank you gifts or trades to the tribes and leaders. Gifts given or traded by potential slave traders to Africans would become monumental to the enslavement process, because the gifts being given were useful and beneficial to the Africans. Sometimes these gifts or trades would include: grains, seasonings, clothing, crafts, and for some tribes the gift of firearms (examples include muskets) would be given for future wars or battles.

A period of developing trust

Trust is an important part of any successful relationship or interaction; especially with people who do not look like you, talk like you, or share the same experiences. However, outsiders, scholars, and potential slave traders could gain a lot of the tribes and leaders trust through consistency and compassion. For example, many outsiders, scholars, and potential slave traders would visit the same tribes frequently and even embrace certain cultural traditions (food, dance, and singing). In addition, some outsiders, scholars, and potential slave traders would participate in certain celebrations, monumental events, and symbolic occasions. In other words, some Africans may have felt that what was valued, loved, and embraced by them was mutually respected and valued by the outsiders/visitors.

A period of advantageousness (divide and conquer)

There is no secret that Africa was not completely unified in terms of tribal affiliations. Warring between African tribes existed, as well as incidents that included the capturing of African prisoners of war (also known as p.o.w.'s). Therefore, benefiting from the current divisions among tribes proved to be another essential part of enslaving Africans. In other words, if certain African tribes are constantly warring with other tribes discussions regarding outsiders/visitors intentions and communications about signs of something being wrong was non-existent. Because communication was non-existent among enemy tribes, no immediate warnings were given regarding neighboring tribes being ambushed, kidnappings, or Africans being shackled, taken, and enslaved. The current divisions, lack of communication, and selective unity among Africans and tribes would serve as an additional and beneficial part of the strategy and enslavement process.

A period of compromise

Making promising offerings is a great tool for deceiving or controlling a person or a group of people. The process of enslaving Africans also included a period of compromise between travelers (potential slave traders) and kings. Potential slave traders would offer kings, tribal leaders, and people of Africa access and exposure to learning about American culture, by taking a return voyage to America. Other potential compromises included exchanging gifts or goods for prisoners of war and indentured servants. Travelers (potential slave traders) would offer gifts or goods in exchange for either p.o.w.'s or indentured servants. In addition, sometimes there was a request that the king of a tribe send tribal some of their tribal warriors to oversee and train the travelers on how to control the prisoners of war and indentured servants; because of potential cultural and language barriers.

The Takeover (chained and headed to America)

Immediately, after arriving into America, the experience and shock for Africans has just begun. Each slave is placed on what is considered *The Block (Auction Block),* and sold to the highest bidder based on certain characteristics and appearances. Some slaves (those with special needs) were sold in the dozens for cheaper prices. Men (specifically young men), women who were barren, women who could have children, lighter skinned women, children, older men, and older women were sold for various prices based on a value system established by the slave market. Africans were no longer allowed to be part of a unified community, but instead Africans were being immediately divided, separated, and sold based on what qualities were valued by potential slave masters, as opposed to how an Africans valued themselves individually and collectively. In other words, Africans new value was based on what was told to them, not what was believed by them.

"Slavery in the United States was much worse than slavery in other countries and had a much more severe effect on the slaves" (The Interactive Journal of Early American Life, Inc., 2001). Slaves were robbed of their cultural history, abused, raped, murdered, controlled by religious doctrine, separated from family and friends, and stripped of all connections to their homeland. The journey from Africa to America was horrific and devastating event that has and continues to mark American history. African culture and traditions were almost decimated, during slavery, while simultaneously destroying personal initiatives and personalities (The Interactive Journal of Early American Life, Inc.,

2001). The impact of the slave era may or may not have a current effect on today's society; depending on one's perceptions and beliefs. No matter one's perception or belief, the fact remains that free Africans became enslaved Americans and were considered property and not human for centuries. "During the slavery era, African Americans were considered chattel, deemed inferior to Whites, and forced into slave labor to support the southern economy (Gabbidon and Greene, 2012).

The process of enslavement is simultaneously perplexing and astonishing because Africans out-numbered slave traders and were familiar with the land. One would think that Africans had the upper hand, when slave traders arrived in Africa. However, the way in which slave traders navigated the land to capture slaves reveals a more sinister truth regarding the enslavement process. Take a moment and think; most of the Africans, who were enslaved, came from tribes that had warriors who were fierce competitors and fighters. Slave traders had develop a strategy to capture Africans; otherwise resistance would occur; especially from the African warriors. Part of the slave traders strategies probably included infiltrating tribes and gathering secretive and relevant information from people within a particular tribe or from enemy tribes who hoped to be spared from slavery. As mentioned in Chapter 1, drums were used for multiple purposes; including communicating secret messages and providing warnings for the Africans. The slave traders who embarked on the soils of Africa were not inexperienced or uninformed about African traditions, the daily occurrences of the people, or the power and connection Africans had with drums. Even though most slave traders could not decipher the drumbeats, slave traders were wise enough to know that whenever Africans were captured all of the drums nearby should be confiscated and burned. Africans always knew the power of the drum, but now slave traders and masters knew, which is why the use of the drum was forbidden along with traditional African dancing, when Africans (slaves) arrived in America and on the plantations.

Whether you agree or disagree with details surrounding the history of slavery, the undisputable truth that bridges all implausibility is that the enslavement of Africans, in America, occurred and its impact lasted for centuries. "As the 17th century closed, it was clear that African slaves were a much better bargain, in terms of costs, [than indentured servants], and the numbers of slaves began to swell. In 1670, Virginia had a population of about 2,000 slaves. By 1708, the number was 12,000" (Wiegand, 2014, p.47). Understanding the implications of slavery beyond the basic concepts of free labor or bartering systems is imperative. The process of enslavement resulted in millions of Africans arriving on the shores of America with more

than just their physical freedom taken.

Chapter 3
From Hopeless to Hopeful: The Power of Spirituals & The Impacts of Lynch, Tubman, and Turner

The reality of slavery was catastrophic and brutally disturbing. Unimaginable pain was done to slaves, which made slaves pray for death rather than endure an unrelenting hell on the plantation. Death was considered a beautiful escape from the constant barrage of torment, as well as escape from white people (Penrice, 2007). Music offered more than just solace for a slave; music offered momentary escape, peace of mind, and an opportunity to express an array of emotions. For those who wanted a more transcendent escape, songs would become essential to their survival. Spirituals were often improvisational, sung acapella, and included a handclap or foot stomp. Spirituals allowed slaves to create a new-life line, since the drum was forbidden in America, because the drum could serve as tool for communication and invigoration of slaves. Spirituals had many

purposes; some of which allowed slaves an opportunity to:

- maintain a level of sanity through oral expression by telling
  stories of hope, praise, love, faith, frustration, protest
  against current beliefs or teachings, struggle, worry, fear,
  hurt, pain, questions to God, sadness, and happiness.
- communicate with one another for the purpose of
  encouragement, expressing one's faith, hope, and desires.
- provide coded messages for slaves to escape, laugh, or
  protest slave teachings.

Spirituals were essential for a slave because these songs allowed

slaves to temporarily escape through a spiritually consciousness.

In other words, even if a slave could not or did not have the

fortitude to escape physically by running away, the songs could

offer a slave solace mentally and spiritually. The purpose of

slavery was more than just acts of abuse or implementing

methods of control for slaves. Slavery was a business, which is why slaves who had musical talent were often valued and sold for more money (Penrice, 2007). Not only did these musically talented slaves work and entertain on the plantation, these talented slaves would be required to entertain the slave master, his family, and friends off the plantation as well.

Slavery was a lucrative business and many slave owners wanted to profit from slavery (free labor) for as long as possible. Whoever could figure out how to keep slaves enslaved forever would become affluent, legendary, and a master of all masters? Ironically, there was such an alleged person; his name is Willie Lynch. Willie Lynch's legend and influence on slavery is not without contradictions. Willie Lynch's existence is indeterminate; leaving many to wonder if Lynch is nothing more than a fictitious person (urban legend) whose loosely adapted 18th century written speech has no historical validity. However, if one chooses to believe or not to believe in the existence of Willie Lynch, the assertions made in the alleged speech is powerful. Lynch's methods for creating a slave mentality that would exits for centuries provides irrefutable evidence of psychological and physiological effects on slaves and future generations.

According to numerous versions of research that supports the existence of Willie Lynch, Lynch is described as British slave owner from the West Indies who would travel from plantation to plantation teaching slave controlling methods; starting specifically in Virginia. Lynch taught crowds of plantation owners and overseers about the best ways to control slaves; as well as introducing the technique, lynching (Morrow, 2003). Lynch was confident beyond conviction that he declared his methods to be full proof and guaranteed to be more effective than traditional slave codes. Slave codes were laws established throughout the United States, embraced criminal law, regulated every aspect of slave life, defined the status of slaves, and the rights of slave owners (Gabbidon and Greene, 2012). For example, specific

slave codes: forbid slaves to read or write, possess weapons,

leave the plantation without the master's permission, lifting a hand

to a white person or making eye contact with a white person,

slaves could not assemble without a white person present, and

marriages between slaves were not binding (Gabbidon and

Greene, 2012).

Allegedly, Willie Lynch would often boast that his

methodology for controlling slaves, if implemented correctly, could

keep Africans enslaved for 300+ years (Morrow, 2003). Even if

slavery ended, the mental enslavement of these Africans would

always exist because Lynch's plan was multi-faceted and

included various methods of physical, mental, emotional, and

spiritual enslavement as well. Willie Lynch's pathology of slavery

allegedly also included suggestive methods for controlling slaves,

which included explaining to slave owners that slaves need to believe in distrust over trust, envy over support, fear over faith and hatred over love. Lynch would also purportedly explained how to divide slaves from one another by valuing slaves differently, based on skills, color, intelligence, age, job title (in-house, field, and slave drivers), and weight (Morrow, 2003).

Another pivotal point of control included causing further dissension among slaves by disrupting the family unit of a slave. Even though slaves' marriages were not considered legally binding, some slaves still chose to marry in a sacred ceremony. Lynch strongly urged the master to be aware of those slaves who chose to marry against the slave codes/rules, because of over-population and the potential rebellion that could occur from a unified family structure. Lynch; therefore, encouraged, the slave master to often separate the husband and wife slaves by having each work in separate areas on the plantation.

Initially, when slave trading began, the majority of slaves that arrived in America were African males and some were indentured servants (McCartney, 2011). Because male slaves, on some plantations, often outnumbered women on plantations, Lynch suggested alternative practices for making money using the male slave. Lynch advised the slave masters to sell the *strong*est slave males seed (semen) to other slave masters who needed to increase their slave populations. Once the slave master made an agreement with another slave master, arrangements were made. The slave male would sleep with other slave women from different plantations for procreation purposes only. Lynch's approach is similar to that of horse breeders. If a male slave is thorough and strong (also known as a thoroughbred), then most likely the male slave will make other thorough and strong children to work on the plantation. The idea of a thoroughbred male slave potentially having strong offspring allowed for the slave master to make more money by selling the slave males seed (semen) to other slave owners.

A slave male (especially a married slave male) having sex outside of marriage and making children with women from different plantations made for constant dissension among married slaves. Eventually, distrust among slave women and any notions of a "piece" of peace or happiness for the enslaved people or their families was destroyed. The attempted bond sometimes forged between a married slave male and woman, in a scenario like this, creates a level of dissension that can never be re-built. The slave male has now potentially created a generation of fatherless children on other plantations that he most likely will never have a relationship with or even see again. Creating dissension within the family structure of slaves allowed for permanent generational dysfunction to occur, which was the purpose of Lynch's methodologies. Willie Lynch also allegedly advised slave owners to occasionally rape female slaves (including the wife of a male slave) (Lynch, 2009). When a slave master rapes a slave woman, the potential for a slave that is a mixture of both races (African and white) could create more profits if the child is mulatto; especially if the child was a girl.

The experience and on-going fear of rape was a constant torment for little girls, young girls, and women alike. Lynch suggested occasional rape, because the rape continues to divide the family causing tension between men and women, fathers and children, mothers and children, and children and children. The division is also destroying the trust between the husband and wife, because when the woman explains that she was raped, the man cannot provide vengeance for her, because it could lead to his own death. The man could also question the woman's love because she did not fight the slave master off; causing the male to wonder if the sex was consensual. Another issue that could arise, should the wife decide not to tell that she was raped, is that the child could be born "too light" showing visible signs of two races (African and White). In other words, the prayer (for the raped female slave), should she not tell, was that the child look African enough to pass as her husband's child. The slave children who were products of a rape that occurred between the slave master and a slave most likely would be raised as being an outcast, never accepted fully by Whites or Africans.

Lastly, Lynch had a specific method to lynching slaves; hence the name lynch. Willie Lynch suggested that beating slaves (whether the reason is legitimate or not) is an important part of the controlling process. Lynch would often suggest that slave owner's occasional beat the strongest and biggest slave in front of the other slaves to create a sense of fear. In addition, Lynch would encourage slave owners to make slaves whip other slaves, to create further division among the group. Should anyone commit an offense that is beyond a redemptive scolding, Lynch suggested the slave be lynched. Allegedly, lynching for Lynch, involved the following process (Lynch, 2009):

Whipping the slave in front of everyone, then tying each limb of the slave to a horse. The slaves and/or overseers would then hit the horses to go in different directions, which would cause the limbs of the slave to rip apart. Afterwards the remaining part of the body, which was the torso would be beaten some more and then hung from a tree and burned, for all of the slaves to see and smell. If the slave master wanted to be vile, he would cut off the genitals.

Lynch's method of lynching was far more gruesome and promoted because he believed the image and smell of burnt flesh would remain engrained in the slaves forever; causing slaves to feel hopeless.

Even though the slaves felt hopeless, faith in God and prayer was able to sustain them until freedom came. For some of the slaves, freedom would come sooner than later in the form of a female; a female named Harriet Tubman. Another pivotal person, who emerged, during the slave era, was a woman by the name of Harriet Tubman. Tubman's birth name Araminta "Minty" Ross and her mother's first name was "Harriet," which is the name she would later adopt as her first name (Bradford, 1961). As a slave, Harriet Tubman lived each day knowing that she could be susceptible to any number of abuses at the hands of the slave master, slave master's wife, the slave master's child(ren), or the overseers. Harriet was as a small framed woman, who could not read or write, but was smart. Some people would probably describe her personality as being "passive-aggressive." Harriet Tubman was passive in the sense that she was never known to be boisterous or outwardly problematic. While enslaved, there is only one notable incident of her outward disobedience. Allegedly, when Harriet was a child, she stole a piece of candy and the slave master hit her over the head for stealing (Sterling, 1970). The punishment given by the slave master would eventually have lasting effects on Harriet, because shortly after being hit on the head, Harriet developed epileptic seizures.

Despite this singular incident, Harriet knew that her life was more than just being a slave. Tubman gathered the strength to escape to freedom; specifically Maryland. Harriet would go on to lead a simple life and get married to John Tubman; hence, the name change (Bradford, 1971). Even though Harriet's freedom was secure, she felt inclined to help others. Harriet's approach to freeing slaves was remarkable as well, because she freed slaves without having to implore violence, which supports the idea of her having "passive" sensibilities. Harriet Tubman and her brothers would eventually risk their lives to go and free other slaves.

Because Tubman was the leader and knew the best time to escape and the best routes to take, she would be eventually be dubbed by slaves (free and enslaved) as "Moses" or "Black Moses." Harriet would never take the same route twice and used varies methods to ensure her and other slaves would be safe. With the help of abolitionists and using a series of passageways (aka The Underground Railroad) Harriet Tubman freed countless people. When asked why she (Harriet) continued to risk her life and overall welfare for others, she responded by saying, "I've freed thousands of slaves, and would have freed thousands more had they known they were slaves" (Bradford, 1961). Harriet Tubman realized (early on) that slavery had paralyzed African people to a point of fear and stagnation. Think about it, slaves outnumbers the slave masters and overseers, yet rarely did rebellions occur. In addition, slaves were not changed and kept in a barn barred from the outside. Slaves walked around on the plantation doing what was told day-in-and-day out and rarely did anyone escape.

Harriet's will and desire to risk her life to save others reveals her selflessness. Harriet was also known to wear a bandana, carry a shotgun, and knife (Conrad, 1942). Most people would assume that the gun and knife were for the slave masters, overseers, or slave catchers. However, those weapons were not just for slave catchers, but mostly for the slaves she was attempting to free. As mentioned in her poignant quote, many slaves would escape, but many people chose to remain slaves; willingly. Unfortunately, some of those who chose to escape with Harriet would begin to develop an increased sense of guilt and trepidation; eventually wanting to stop or go back to the plantation. This level of guilt and trepidation could threaten the overall mission of the escape. Harriet could not allow anyone to jeopardize her life and the lives of the people she was trying to free. Sometimes she would have to show her shotgun or knife and urge anyone who wanted to stop or go back to the plantation, because the risk to return outweighed the risk of continuing. Imaginatively, Tubman may have responded by saying, "Either keep it moving or lie where you stand," revealing her "aggressive sensibilities" and desire to not let anyone jeopardize the overall mission and goals. Harriet Tubman is the epitome of what Hip Hop culture would call an O.G. (Original.Gangster.). Her life, struggles, sacrifices, and willingness to free and protect others (strangers) makes her legendary. Spiritual songs like *Moses*, were most likely reflective of her experiences helping slaves escape to freedom.

Another influential person, during the slave era was a man by the name of Nat Turner. Nat Turner was born a slave and served as a tradesman on the plantation. Aside from his duties on the plantation, Nat Turner was a preacher, as well. One day while sleeping, Turner, claimed to have received an epiphany from God, which revealed that the serpent is loose and needs to be killed (Gray, 1831). Turner interpreted these words to mean that the slave master, the slave master's wife, and the slave master's child(ren) would need to be killed. Turner along with four other men would plan the revolt on July 4, 1831 (Gray, 1831). However, after Turner became ill, he changed the date to August 21, 1831 (Bisson, 2005). One would think that being sick was sign from God not to commit murder; however, Turner took his illness graciously, believing that he would now be at full strength to lead a rebellion. Nat Turner followed the interpretation of his epiphany and killed the master, the master's wife, and the master's child(ren) (Bisson, 2005).

Typically, in war, women and children are spared; however, as heartless, demonic, and murderous as Turner's actions were, his decision from a psychosomatic position was purposeful. Nat Turner realized the evilness of slavery was generationally influenced. In other words, the potential for abuse was just as inherent within the slave masters' family, just as victimization and fear became inherent to slaves. The same dysfunctional relationships that occurred between male slaves and female slaves (especially those slaves who were married) were replicated in the slave master's relationship with his wife. The slave master's wife, in many cases, was aware of her husband's adulterous behavior, which included the raping of slave women. Because of the awareness, sometimes the slave master's wife would verbally and physically abuse the female slave. The slave master's wife would also treat the female slave with harsh acts of retribution, which may include selling her children to neighboring plantations or requiring the female slave to do extra work. The slave master's wife might even resort to occasionally raping a male slave to ignite jealousy from the slave master. Unfortunately, the worse abusers on the plantation would often be at the hands of the slave master's child(ren). The slave master's child(ren) would be heinously worse, in comparison to the parents, because the slave master's child(ren) knew about the infidelity issues, the cross-breeding, and embarrassment of half-siblings. The slave master's child(ren) would often have a ravenous rage and hatred towards both female and male slaves. Many slave masters' families were comprised of former and potential future slave owners who believed in the continuation of slavery; therefore, Nat Turner believed that in order for slavery to end every aspect of the slavery must be destroyed. He believed that all members of the slave master's family needed to be killed including women and children.

Because of Nat Turner's thought process and actions, Turner is the *original* epitome of what Tupac coined as the T.H.U.G.L.I.F.E. philosophy. Tupac Shakur was more than just a rapper and his talent and acuity proved that he was intelligent. In 1992, Tupac Shakur tattooed his stomach and revealed a new perceptual concept called T.H.U.G.L.I.F.E. The term was chagrin to most people, who assumed that the tattoo and the concept was gang related and dismissed Tupac's concept. However, the concept was not a gang infused notion, but one of reflection. The concept T.H.U.G.L.I.F.E. would become an acronym for truth. The concept, which is also tattooed on Tupac's stomach, stood for "The. Hate. U. Give. Little. Infants. F**ks. Everyone". In other words, Tupac, like others, realized that children come into this world developing learned behaviors that have a negative impact on the child, who then turns and directs that hate towards everyone else. Tupac's sentiments, in 1990, would be the same sentiments that sparked the Nat Turner Rebellion.

Even though, Nat Turner's rebellion would be historically infamous, deemed ineffective by local newspapers, his death considered meaningless by slave masters, Turner's reasoning would be deemed purposeful and logical, by future generations. Even though Nat Turner's rebellion resulted in the deaths of men, women, and children, Nat Turner did not act without some level of consciousness. Turner's goal was not to kill *all* white people, *only* those whites who owned slaves (Gray, 1831). While leading the revolt, Turner, did encounter other white families, but those families were spared because they did not own slaves. Nat Turner's legacy is wrought with conflictions of what constitutes justice. The essence of Nat Turner's spirit can be found in rap lyrics, graffiti, and tattoos. Most people may have noticed Tupac Shakur's huge tattoo of the Christian cross on his back; however, few people may have realized that within the cross was a significant word and year. The word "Exodus," which is symbolic of the story of Moses freeing slaves, in the Bible, and the year "1831," which is the year of Nat Turner's rebellion. In addition to the tattooed cross on his back, Tupac also rapped songs like, *Only God Can Judge Me* (1996). The song lyrics, of Tupac, reveal how struggle, pain, stress, paranoia, and fear can make someone wish for death rather than pray for change; similar to some slave spirituals sung by slaves.

Despite Willie Lynch's destructive strategies of enslavement, slaves were given additional choices to seek freedom by way of Harriet Tubman or Nat Turner's methods. Whether people opted to plan a secret escape or lead a revolt, one's faith in God was pivotal for a slave's existence. Slaves could create an unimaginable level of strength through faith and could remain as hopeful as possible; despite the daily realities of life. Having the ability to sing spirituals inspired slaves to endure. Spirituals have different categories and themes; which includes protest songs, work and field songs, encouraging and hopeful songs, tragic songs, coded-songs, escape songs, and humorous songs. Each spiritually themed song had relevance; especially to those singing; however, coded songs were uniquely significant, because these songs often included secrets messages that slaves did not want the masters, overseers, or disloyal slaves to understand.

Many whites were unaware of the value of spirituals to slaves or that coded messages existed within spiritual lyrics. The deeper meaning behind the spirituals was not revealed until after 1867 (two years after the Emancipation Proclamation) publication of *Slave Songs of the United States*. The Spirituals, including coded message songs, would be recorded and popularized by the Fisk Jubilee singers, starting on October 6, 1871, which has become a commemorative date called Jubilee Day (Reavis, 1995). Lead by the Fisk Treasurer, George L. White, the original Fisk Jubilee singers included a nine-member group, which included: Isaac Dickerson, Maggie Porter, Minnie Tate, Jennie

Jackson, Benjamin Holmes, Thomas Rutling, Eliza Walker, Green Evans, and Ella Sheppard (Reavis, 1995).

Two distinct examples of songs that were relevant, during slavery, which provided a theme of protest and a coded message for escape were songs called *Heav'n Heav'n* (also known as *I Got Shoes...*) and *Moses*. The lyrical content in the song, *Heav'n Heav'n*, is reflective of the slaves' resistance to the slave masters teachings. Slave masters and overseers would use religion (specifically Christianity) as a tool of oppression against slaves. Slave masters would use multiple methods to control and constantly remind slaves that slavery is justified and part of God's will. Techniques and teachings included, but were not limited to the following:

- Slave masters would remove scriptural books from the Bible such as Exodus.

- Slave masters would uses specific scriptures (Ephesians 6:5, 1 Peter 2:18, 1 Timothy 6:1-2, Colossians 3: 22-25, Titus 2:9) from the Bible to justify slavery.
- Slave masters would constantly remind slaves that neither life nor death would serve as an escape from slavery. The slaves masters taught slaves that their heaven was called *Nigger Heaven*. *Nigger Heaven* was the balcony of the church where slaves sat, when attending church with the slave master. *Nigger Heaven* was also known as a slave masters name for where slaves go when they die. According to the slave master's teachings, *Nigger Heaven* was segregated (by a gate) and reserved for obedient slaves only. The slave master would teach the slaves that once in *Nigger Heaven*, the slave would experience "heaven from a distance." Heaven, for a slave, was being able to look through a peep hole of the segregated gate in heaven and see the slave master and other white people, in all of their glory, which includes crowns, robes, and shoes. A slaves heaven was seeing White people, including their masters be treated like royalty, but never

able to experience. In other words, heaven for a slave was being able to "look, but not enjoy."

To combat these false teachings, some slaves created specific spirituals to combat the slave masters teachings. These spirituals are called protest songs. The song, *Heav'n, Heav'n* (also known as *I Got Shoes, You Got Shoes*) lyrics are as follows:

I got a robe, you got a robe,
All God's children got a robe.
When I get to Heav'n gonna put on my robe,

Gonna shout all over God's Heav'n, Heav'n, Heav'n
Everybody talkin' bout Heav'n ain't going there,
Heav'n, Heav'n, Heav'n.
Gonna shout all over God's Heav'n.

I got shoes, you got shoes,
All God's children got shoes.
When I get to Heav'n gonna put on my shoes,

Gonna walk all over God's Heav'n, Heav'n, Heav'n

Everybody talkin' bout Heav'n ain't going there,

Heav'n, Heav'n, Heav'n.

Gonna shout all over God's Heav'n.

I got a harp, you got a harp,

All God's children got a harp.

When I get to Heav'n gonna play on my harp,

Gonna play all over God's Heav'n, Heav'n, Heav'n

Everybody talkin' bout Heav'n ain't going there,

Heav'n, Heav'n, Heav'n.

Gonna shout all over God's Heav'n.

Contrary to popular belief, slaves were aware of the basic

principles of Christianity prior to becoming a slave, in America.

Various African tribes had prior spiritual beliefs about what

happens when you die. Africans believed that you are born, then

you and die; after you die you are buried and after you are buried,

you rise through resurrection.

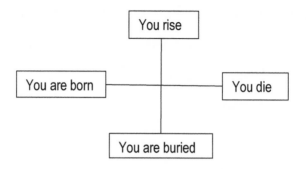

Ironically, the Africans beliefs were symbolically manifested in the same symbol as the Christian cross. Africans' spiritual beliefs about life after death, as well as burial and resurrection beliefs were enhanced after some African people learned about the life experiences of Jesus Christ from travelling Christian missionaries.

Because slave codes prevented slaves from reading and writing, slaves had to develop a way to pass down information and inspiration without the slave masters or overseers knowing. Slaves would had prior knowledge would teach other slaves about the aspects of the Bible that was hidden by the slave masters; specifically Exodus. Some slave masters and overseers allegedly removed books like the Exodus from the Bibles on the plantation and at church, just in case a slave tried to open and read the Bible.

Another protest song that slaves created, was a song called *Moses*. The song is relevant and reveals slaves prior knowledge of the Bible, prior to slavery. Insight about Jesus, Moses, and other biblical characters experiences and triumphs had significant meaning to a slave and offered inspiration for slaves to endure. Take a moment to read the sample song and begin to ask yourself (without the use of research tools) what these lyrics mean and why the song includes a lot of repetition. The lyrics to the spiritual *Moses* is as follows:

> Moses, Moses, don't you let King Pharaoh overtake you,
> Moses, Moses, don't you let King Pharaoh overtake you,
> Moses, Moses, don't you let King Pharaoh overtake you,
> In some lonesome graveyard.

Hm, hm, I hear the chariot comin,'
Hm, hm, I hear the chariot comin,'
Hm, hm, I hear the chariot comin,'
In some lonesome graveyard.

Moses, Moses, I hear the horses' runnin,'
Moses, Moses, I hear the horses' runnin,'
Moses, Moses, I hear the horses' runnin,'
In some lonesome graveyard.

Hm, hm, I hear Jordan rollin,'
Hm, hm, I hear Jordan rollin,'
Hm, hm, I hear Jordan rollin,'
In some lonesome graveyard.
Mother, mother, don't you let your daughter condemn you,
Mother, mother, don't you let your daughter condemn you,
Mother, mother, don't you let your daughter condemn you,
In some lonesome graveyard.

Hm, hm, I hear the angels moaning,
Hm, hm, I hear the angels moaning,
Hm, hm, I hear the angels moaning,

In some lonesome graveyard.

Jordan, Jordan, let the children over,
Jordan, Jordan, let the children over,
Jordan, Jordan, let the children over,
In some lonesome graveyard.

Hopefully, after reading the lyrics, you notice the repetition of certain phrases/words; as the phrasing of certain words can determine which words may serve as code words or warnings for slaves singing and listening to the song. The song, *Moses*, is considered a coded escape song, because the song includes a reference to an Old Testament biblical character; Moses, who was responsible for freeing slaves. The song, *Moses*, also follows the exact same storyline as that of the Old Testament regarding Moses' mission to help free Hebrew slaves from the reign and tyranny of the Egyptian Pharaohs.

Slaves experienced life in an almost identical way as the biblical characters; therefore the songs message and inspiration was heightened. For example, in the Bible, the Israelites were God's children who had become enslaved by an oppressor. The Israelites yearned to be rescued from their daily torment. Eventually, Moses (figuratively and biblically), would become pivotal to their freedom. Other noteworthy biblical character names that have become synonymous with spiritual songs are Gabriel, Isaiah, and Jesus. However, the song, *Moses*, is particularly significant and important for slaves, because the song reveals the on-going danger, fear, guilt, mental anguish and potential punishment associated with escaping. Key biblical characters and words that have significant meaning, in songs like *Moses, Sometimes I Feel, Like A Motherless Child*, or *Swing Low Sweet Chariot* include coded names and words like: Moses, King

Pharaoh, mother, daughter, Jordan, chariot, birds, trains, angels, motherless, and home.

When discussing the purpose of Hip Hop culture, the original purpose for the movement was to be a "voice for the voiceless." Before one can become "the voice for the voiceless," one must know the history of the voiceless. Hip Hop music, specifically rap, is recently more known for having a brash and braggadocious attitude with heavy beat oriented sounds amid low lyrical content that often describes violence, anti-love, anti-government, and aggressive language. However, one must consider an alternative perspective when discussing the effects of slavery. What if today's rap music is simply an evolved reflection of slave history that was never fully addressed or corrected because former slaves and descendants of slaves never received true redemption? The essence of Hip Hop culture is centered on the ability to freely express one's self; whether it be in the form of dj'ing, fashion, clothes, work, lyrics, videos, music, graffiti, beatboxing, writing, or business entrepreneurship.

Rap lyrics have can reveal an array of emotions (ranging from positive-to-negative-to indifferent), experiences, and struggles for an artists, just as spirituals did for slaves. Often times rappers' lyrics will seem identical to an experience that a slave could live or similar to an emotion a slave could have felt. Instead of coded messages, current day rappers often rely on the use of metaphors, double entendres, and first-hand accounts of struggle to express meaning and relevance. Two specific examples of artists that reflect the connection between Spirituals and modern day rap lyrics are Jay-Z and Tupac Shakur. The first example, includes, Jay-Z's song, *Heaven* (2013), says:

> Arm, leg, leg, arm, head – this is God body/ Knowledge, wisdom, freedom, understanding, we just want our equality/ Food, clothing, shelter, help a nigga find some peace/ Happiness for a gangster, ain't no love in these

streets/ Question religion, question it all/ Question existence until them questions are solved/

[Bridge: Jay-Z]
That's me in the corner, that's me in the spotlight...Losing my religion, losing my religion

[Verse 2]
Getting ghost in the Ghost/ Can you see me? Can you see me?/ And God is my chauffeur, boy they love Hova/ Tell that preacher he's a preacher/ I'm a mo****f*****g prophet/ Smoke a tree of knowledge, drink from a gold chalice/ You gotta love it/ I arrive at the pearly gates I had luggage/ meaning I had baggage/ Niggas asking me questions/ I don't answer to these busters/ Only God could judge us, mo****f****r, uh/

Jay-Z's lyrics, in the song, *Heaven*, includes multiple metaphors and double entendres (similar to code words) regarding the concept of heaven. What is also dualistically noteworthy to this discussion is how life can become overwhelming causing one to question everything, including one's faith in religion and the preacher. Jay-Z's verse continues to reveal that if those preaching are true preachers, then he is a prophet, a person who sees unadulterated truth. Consequently, these experiences lead Jay-Z to want to disappear from the stressors of life, when he says getting' ghost in the ghost, while simultaneously making reference to ghost, as in Holy ghost, which allows for believers to experience an outer body spiritual experience, while still existing in the present.

The second rap song example, includes, Tupac Shakur's song, *Only God Can Judge Me (1996)*. Tupac says:

Is it a crime, to fight, for what is mine?/ Everybody's dyin'/ tell me what's the use of tryin'/ I've been trapped since birth, cautious, cause I'm cursed/ And fantasies of my family, in a hearse/ And they say it's the white man I should fear/ But, it's my own kind doin' all the killin' here/ I can't lie, ain't no love for the other side/ Jealousy inside, make em wish I died/ Oh my

Lord, tell me what I'm livin' for/ Everybody's droppin' got me knockin' on heaven's door/

These rap lyrics, written and performed by Tupac Shakur, in 1996, could be reminiscent of an experience from a slave living in America, in 1776. The reality of slave life included more death and abuse than escape, as well as an inescapable fear about everyday life, which makes some people want to die and go to heaven. Tupac's words share the same sentiments as some slaves. Some slaves captured during the Middle Passage, as well as slaves who experienced life on the plantation were willing to take their own life, rather than endure slavery. Tupac's final line in the last verse, shows some irony, in that he is feeling so much pressure that he wants to go to Heaven now.

Unfortunately, the notion of knocking on Heaven's door, suggests that Heaven's door is not open or a place where you can just walk in.

Another important aspect of slave life that was an unfortunate reality was the divisions that existed among the enslaved. The methods of slavery were created for optimal control and for purposes of dividing, not uniting. Therefore, there is no surprise that snitching and hatred for slaves would not just extend from the masters or overseers, but from one slave to another slave. Having to deal with the mental, spiritual, and physical bondages of slavery from white slave owners and overseers was an already overwhelming experience. However, having to deal with other slaves reciprocating these same ideas, beliefs, and behaviors towards one another was demoralizing. All of these emotions as well as lingering questions about why God would allow such injustice and mistreatment to occur were major themes in a slave's life; but also expressed in several spirituals sung by slaves.

Chapter 4
Sold Out, But Not Necessarily a Sell-Out

The history of the Minstrel Shows, which *initially* included White performers painting their faces with burnt cork to mimic slaves, was a controversially entertaining era in American history. The Minstrel Show blackface performances, by many accounts, are considered the first popularized American art form of entertainment. The Minstrel Shows emerged during the Industrial Revolution period of 1820, in New York (Sweet, 2000). Typical research reveals Dan Emmett, Billy Whitlock, Dick Pelham, Frank Brower, Joel Sweeny, George Dixon, and E.P. Christy as major contributors to the Minstrel Shows. E.P. Christy would be known for evolving the Minstrel Show, into a three-act structure, in the 1840s and 1850s, involving the following (Strausbaugh, 2006):

1) A host called Mr. Interlocutor and two blackface comedians (often Brudder Bones and Brudder Tambo) who would do walkarounds, sing songs, and the cakewalk dance (a competitive dance performed by slaves for slave masters, resulting in the winner receiving a cake).

2) An olio, which was a speech about slaves, slave life, or politics.

3) A comedic musical plantation skit, which included slave characters, slave music, and slave dance. These skits would eventually grow into full-length shows.

Even though other people contributed to the Minstrel Shows, Thomas Dartmouth Rice (aka Daddy Rice) is considered the Father of the Minstrel Shows. Rice is the genius behind the Daddy Rice character and the Jump Jim Crow song and dance phenomenon that spread locally and internationally (Cockrell, 1997). The shows content was considered entertaining to audiences despite the mocking of immigrant groups like the Irish, Germans, and Jews (Sweet, 2000). Free slaves were mocked as well; however, slaves were the primary targets of the shows

offensive humor. The Minstrel Shows became legendary with the

incorporation of stereotypical characterizations of slaves and

slave life. Even though the show's top character was Jim Crow,

the shows included additional such as the Mulatto, Wench,

Mammy, Uncle Tom, Dandy, Young Buck, Zip Coon, Sambo,

(Brudder) Bones, and (Brudder) Tambo. Some of these

characters like Dandy, Zip Coon, Mulatto, Wench, Young Buck,

Mammy, and Uncle Tom would later be transformed into the

mediatization of characters, who become known as the: Uppity

Negro, Pimp, Redbone, Ho, and Thug, as well as merchandise

branding products like Aunt Jemima pancakes and Uncle Ben's

rice. The elements of the Minstrel Show are consistent with

historical accounts; however, the creation and creator of these

highly successful shows are questionable.

Knowing and understanding the dynamics that created the

Minstrel Shows is not only important to understanding Hip Hop

culture's history, but American history; especially as it relates to

entertainment. To understand the history of the Minstrel Shows,

three questions must be explored: *Why* were the shows started?,

What initially inspired the shows creation?, and *Who* originated

the shows? These three questions will provide foundational

information about the true history of the Minstrel Shows and

determine whether the American entertainment has changed or

remained the same.

The Minstrel Shows were in existence throughout the late

1700s, in places like New York. However, the shows began to

peak around the early 1800s; specifically 1820s, when the

American Industrial Revolution started (Sweet, 2000). Because of

the effects of the Industrial Revolution, the potential for

apprenticeships were destroyed and the invention of machines reduced jobs. In other words, master craftsmen, prior to the Industrial Revolution, would offer apprenticeship opportunities to young people, the young people would then become journeymen and earn a lucrative living (Sweet, 2000). Unfortunately, when the Industrial Revolution occurred, the master craftsmen received all the available jobs, which flooded the job market, and left many young people with either a lower paying job or no job at all. The lack of employment opportunities, in places like New York, caused many young people; especially thousands of African (free) and Irish American laborers to struggle to survive (Sweet, 2000). To survive, some African and Irish Americans became gangsters and participated in illegal activities to make money, while others began to use drugs, started drinking, or started entertaining on the street for money, food, or drink as means to cope or survive.

Shivaree is a unique musical term that has cultural significance throughout the world. Historically, Shivarees are described as a raucous musical-sketch performance led by a group of unmarried, unemployed, drunk young men, who dressed in outlandish costumes; while singing and dancing in the streets (Sweet, 2000). The performances were often conducted, in upper class neighborhoods, with the purposes of receiving money, food, or drink as compensation (Sweet, 2000). The traditions and performances varied depending on one's ethnicity. For example, Italians' version of Shivarees is called Charivari, Spanish-Caribbeans' version is called Aguinaldo, and Black-West Indians' version is called John Canoe (Sweet, 2000). Performing Shivarees were often beneficial for the performers; in that "low-call society turned the world upside down without lawful penalties" (Sweet, 2000). Even though the performances were somewhat entertaining, sometimes the performances were a nuisance for neighbors.

During the Industrial Revolution (1820s), Shivarees were

revived, within the local communities, because people needed

employment, money, and food, while still desiring a sense of

enjoyment and entertainment. In New York, the top local

performers were Black and Irish Americans (Sweet, 2000).

Ironically, the Africans and Irish Shivaree performances included

the same theatrical premise and characters: a king, the villain

(aka the evil one), the doctor, and the hero (Sweet, 2000). The

story plot for each musical-sketch performance was brief and

incorporated cultural dance styles, lingual accents, and social

mannerisms. In other words, when the Africans performed their

cultural traditions were included in the performance, which

included multi-movement dancing, ring-shout songs, and buckling

knees and shuffling feet (Sweet, 2000). When the Irish

performed, their cultural traditions were included in the

performance, which included jig-dancing, hornpipes music, and high leg lifts (Sweet, 2000). Even though African (multi-movement) and Irish (Irish jig) dance styles differed, both cultural performances included the same storyline (Sweet, 2000):

The villain (dressed in black) tries to kill the king (dressed royal garb with a crown), but is stopped by the hero. The hero (dressed in red, purple, and blue with a sword) is slain, while saving the king's life. Then at the king's request, the doctor (dressed in white) resurrects the hero, who retaliates and kills the villain.

Even though African and Irish Americans performed Shivarees in different locations, sometimes the two groups would visit the same local taverns to drink, party, and have fun (Sweet, 2000). As each group would drank more and more, impromptu musical performances would occur; allowing Africans and Irish people to be exposed to one another's cultural traditions.

Unfortunately, with each drink that flowed, at the local tavern, the potential for offenses heightened between the African and Irish Americans. Rumors suggest that one evening; some Irish American Shivaree performers arrived at one of the local taverns drunk and started to mock African traditions by making ape sounds, shuffling their feet, speaking in broken dialect; all while in blackface. In response to the Irish American's performance, in the local tavern, some of the African Shivaree performers immediately responded to the offenses by doing an Irish jig and making hornpipe sounds. Allegedly, a fight immediately broke out at the local tavern and ignited mockery to ensue between African and Irish Shivaree performers. For weeks, both groups performed their Shivarees, not just in the upper class neighborhoods, but now locally with these newly included cultural insults. However, both Shivaree traditions (African & Irish) would now include new elements.

The Irish Shivaree would now depict the villain in blackface with a black wig, while making the villain dance outlandishly and uncontrollably to banjo music; like Africans were perceived to dance (Cockrell, 1997). Africans also revised their Shivaree performances. The villain, in the African version, would now have a white painted face and dance in an Irish jig to fiddle music; like Irish were perceived to dance (Sweet, 2000). Eventually, both groups would be arrested countless times for disturbing the peace without a performance license (Sweet, 2000). Performers, from both groups (African and Irish), sometimes would actually receive more money, drink, or food, because of the newly revised performances (Sweet, 2000).

The local Shivaree performances (African and Irish), in spite of performers being arrested for disturbing the peace, were becoming comically popular among the locals and upper class. However, the performances were always random and impromptu.

The potential success of these shows were evident, but the current organization of the shows were disorganized. There is an eerie old saying, "Somebody is always watching you." This saying would become true, when it comes to the discussion of "Who" created the Minstrel Shows.

Thomas Dartmouth "Daddy" Rice, who was born on the lower east side of Manhattan, New York, is considered the "Father of Minstrel Shows." However, Rice's title as "Father of the Minstrel Shows" is somewhat questionable. In other words, should the first person to promote a new idea be given more credit than the person who invented the idea? Thomas Dartmouth "Daddy" Rice is credited with creating the Minstrel Shows and popularizing the Minstrel Show character "Jim Crow," in 1828, in a New York City theatre (Strausbaugh, 2006). However, history reveals that the character "Jim Crow" had a long tradition rooted in African culture. In fact, some of the history, surrounding the name Jim Crow, is connected with:

- African folktales, which included a crow named Jim Crow
- A stolen song and dance called Jump Jim Crow, from a crippled old man named Jim Crow
- Segregation laws called Jim Crow

One of the initial connections the name Jim Crow has is a connection to African folklore. African folklore often includes many references to animals to help emphasize stories and experiences. For example, the movie, *The Lion King*, had several African traditions, proverbs, and animals to signify certain characteristics. The crow in African folklore personifies deceptiveness and is synonymous with a black bird (Terres, 1980). "Along the seaboard of the southeastern states and

Yoruba culture in West Africa, the vernacular name for black bird is Jim" (Abrahams, 1985 and Sweet, 2000).

A secondary connection with the term Jim Crow relates to the controversial history of how Thomas Dartmouth Rice developed the stage name, dance, and song called Jump Jim Crow. Some research asserts that Jim Crow was not a real person, but an archetype for slaves and slave life. Other research reveals that Rice stole the name of his character, the clothes, the dance, and the song from an actual slave named Jim Crow Daddy (Loft, 1993). The story surrounding the theft of "Jim Crow" is described as follows, according to some researched accounts. Thomas Dartmouth Rice met an old black man, with a crooked leg and deformed shoulder named Jim Crow, who was performing a dance and a song called "Jumping Jim Crow" for money (Loft, 1993). Rice was amazed at the performance and believed the audiences who attended his Minstrel Shows would love this new addition to the show. Rice *supposedly* paid the old man for his clothes and to teach him the dance and the song. The Jump Jim Crow song included the following lyrics:

Come listen all you galls and boys
I'se jist from Tuckyhoe,
I'm goin to sing a little song,
My name is Jim Crow

Fist on de heel tap,
Den on the toe
Ebry time I weel about
I jump Jim Crow.
Weel about and turn about
En do jus so,
And every time I weel about,
I jump Jim Crow.

Once, Rice perfected the song, dance, and mannerisms, he introduced the new character at his show. After performing, his new act, Thomas Dartmouth Rice's career catapulted him into fame. Rice traveled locally and abroad making him the highest paid Minstrel Show performer and an international star. Did Thomas D. Rice the dubbed "Father of the Minstrel Shows' create, adapt, or steal the character "Jim Crow" and the song and dance "Jump Jim Crow? Has history evolved in such a way that the original creator of Minstrel Shows a myth or does character adaptation count as innovatively authentic, in the world of entertainment?

The final connection with the term Jim Crow is synonymous with the law; specifically the Jim Crow law. The Jim Crow law's, were established in 1890. The basic premise of the law was "separate, but equal." Ironically, those (specifically Blacks) who lived during the height of the Jim Crow law quickly realized that the Jim Crow actually promoted a notion of "separate and *un*equal." Jim Crow laws served as a loophole, in the law, for

100

people who endorsed racism, segregation, and prejudice. Unfortunately, the Jim Crow law was upheld; especially in southern states, longer than one may have wanted. The name of the law (Jim Crow) speaks of equality, while simultaneously limiting equality is baffling. How can one have faith in any law that is named after a deceptive African folklore character or a Minstrel show character whose reputation is founded in stereotypical mockery and jokes? Sarcastically speaking, the joke was on people of color; specifically Black people, who would believe in any law that was conjured in deception would create change for the better. The thought of an actual law that affects people's lives has roots in such a controversial era is unsettling.

The Industrial Revolution, ironically, coincided with Thomas D. Rice's rise to Minstrel Show fame. When watching or listening to audio of these performances, from a historical standpoint, one could easily determine where these elements came from; especially the exaggerated depictions and mannerism associated with slavery and slave life. These subtle revelations about who should be credited as the true originator and who benefitted from the shows the most. This revelation eventually led Blacks to create their own Minstrel Shows, around the 1860s and 1870s, which would become known as "The Authentic Minstrel Shows," by Black Minstrel Show performers (Toll, 1974). The creation of an all-Black Minstrel Show cast was controversially inspiring. Controversial, because Blacks were painting their faces in burnt cork, adapting to a typecasting formula, and perpetuating the same stereotypes that White performers promoted. Inspiring, because the shows were successful and Black people were afforded an opportunity to work (escape plantation life), make money, lead to other job opportunities like acting, travel, and become famous. While Black performers took over travelling Minstrel Shows, White blackface performers shifted to becoming Vaudeville performers. Vaudeville is a form of entertainment that includes various elements, such as blackface, music, acrobats, dancers, comedians, trained animals, lectures, movies, impersonators, one-act plays, singing, magicians, trapeze artists, jugglers, and athletes (S.D., 2006).

Because of the controversial popularity surrounding the Minstrel Shows, two contrasting views seemed to always emerge. The two differing perceptions could be summarized in the quotes of Frederick Douglass and Mark Twain. Frederick Douglass declares, "Blackface performers are,...the filthy scum of white society, who have stolen from us a complexion denied them by nature, in which to make money, and pander to the corrupt taste of their white fellow citizens" (Douglass, 1848). However, Mark Twain states that "If I could have the nigger show back again in its pristine purity, I should have little use for opera" (Twain, 1917). These two perceptions (Douglass' and Twains') expose a level of tension that caused many to wonder the following: Where is the line drawn between entertainment and reality? In other words, if stereotypical comedy and mockery equals lucrative entertainment, then what price has a culture paid for being caricaturized and mocked? For Douglass, white performers who participated in blackface were pitiful degenerates who depicted slavery imagery for profit. However, Douglass was even more enraged, when Negros began to perform in blackface shows, because of the history and potential futuristic effect on the characterization of Black people.

There is an old entertainment cliché, "If it is funny, then it should be in showbiz." Dualistically, this same notion can be interpreted as saying that if you laugh at any aspect of a show that includes stereotypical comedy, then you erase the offense. In other words, you cannot watch Minstrel Shows or any comical performances and be both entertained and offended at the same time. Understanding this reality can be somewhat confusing for audiences. For example, if I laugh at an offensive joke or statement about someone from another culture am I innocently laughing because of the humor in the offense? Or, am I laughing because I actually believe what is being said? Because I laughed, does that mean that I am secretly stereotyping people and promoting prejudices? Lastly, am I laughing because I am possibly a conscious or unconscious racist? Each of these questions can make anyone uncomfortable; however, when someone makes the same joke or statement at a comedic event, the rules seem to change. In other words, is comedic entertainment exempt from laws of truths? Also, are falsities or offenses that may arise during comedic performances irrelevant in the world of entertainment? When you listen to the latest rap song or video, what do you notice? Is this just entertainment? Are the lyrics exaggerated for humor and nonsensical purposes?

Are you offended by the words or the depictions in the video? These questions are not meant to make one feel remorseful, guilty, judged, or trigger an outrage or outright rejection of comedy or entertainment. However, understanding the history of why people are or are not offended could have deep roots to the Minstrel Show period.

The Minstrel Shows success and the creation of an all-Black Minstrel Show was created because there were a number of supporters who did not find the show offensive enough to ban the show. Entertainment success is not determined by who is offended but by the financial gains achieved. In the words of Jay-Z, "Men lie, women lie, numbers don't." Many people may not agree with Minstrel Shows or the stereotypes promoted because of the historic implications of offense. However, one cannot deny the dualistic complexities of an era like the Minstrel Shows. The Minstrel Show perpetuated dualistic purposes in promoting stereotypical imagery of slaves, while simultaneously providing

opportunities for slaves and eventually freed slaves to gain a

sense of notoriety and success. Performing in Minstrel Shows,

afforded some slaves and opportunity to temporarily escape

plantation life and be applauded for once rather than abused.

Whether you believe Thomas Dartmouth "Daddy" Rice is the

authentic creator and proprietor of the Minstrel Shows or you

believe African and/or Irish people were the creators, the impact

of these shows are ever-present and continues to create racial

divides and controversy; especially in Hip Hop culture. The

Minstrel Show era's creation and success made New York one of

the premier entertainment cities, in America. Evoking the saying,

"If you can make it in New York, you can make it anywhere."

Chapter 5

The Harlem Renaissance: Short-Lived With Long-Term Impacts

The Great Migration, which started at the beginning of the 20th century, had a tremendous impact in the lives of West Indians, Africans, American Negroes, and those who migrated from the south to places like Harlem, New York. The Harlem Renaissance became an essentially idealistic movement, because the movement would allow for a sense of re-awakening, re-birth, and re-defining period for the newly emancipated slaves and the Negro culture. The Harlem Renaissance was a literary inspired movement that promoted multiculturalism through various forms of artistic expression. Information varies on the specific start date and how long the movement lasted. However, one essential date is considered monumental to the movement. On

March 21, 1924 at the Civic Club a dinner was held for the Harlem Renaissance stakeholders.

The Civic Club Dinner was organized by visionaries like Alain LeRoy Locke and Charles S. Johnson and included a bevy of influential and affluent leaders. The Civic Club Dinner helped create and cultivate various beneficial relationships between Whites, Jews, and Blacks, while simultaneously endorsing the talents of painters, musicians, poets, publishers, actors, educators, authors, comedians, and leaders. This new venture and opportunity helped establish crucial business relationships through networking. Patrons and artists attending the Civic Club Dinner were able to connect, converse, and develop a strategic plan for inclusion. Patrons and artists were also able to promote alternative aspects and perceptions of black culture; using various artistic expressions starting specifically with literature.

Interestingly, cultivating multicultural business relationships was still difficult to maintain; as the attempt to unify people at the Civic Club Dinner, coincided with on-going segregation, racism, inequality, and continual lynchings. In other words, even though slavery was abolished and Blacks migrated to the north, the same issues, frustrations, and attacks still existed. The Harlem Renaissance provided an alternative perspective of black culture and also allowed Whites, Irish, Jews, and Latinos to experience first-hand relationships that revealed evolved variations of black talent and intelligence. Before the Harlem Renaissance, most Whites had limited interactions and perceptions about Black people, because of the lack of first-hand experiences and interactions, continuous negative stereotypes, and misperceived notions about the academic intelligence of Blacks. In addition, the derogatory imagery depicted during the Minstrel Show era created additional negative misperceptions and mischaracterizations. Everyone (good, bad, or indifferent), who attended the Civic Club Dinner, as well as later contributors to the movement are essential to the creation, existence, and futuristic impact of the Harlem Renaissance.

Patrons, artists, and supporters were all critical to the Harlem Renaissance's relevance, impact, and foundation; however, decision to choose Harlem as the location for the movement was just as significant. For example, Harlem was a prime location for establishing and cultivating talent, but also for promoting cultural diversity. Coincidentally, New York, especially during the days of Thomas D. Rice's Minstrel Shows, was considered the "mecca of entertainment." In other words, there should be no surprise that some of the most prolific thinkers, talents, and writers began to migrate from down south to up north and emigrate from other countries to New York; specifically Harlem. Harlem; specifically, in the early 1900s served as a melting pot for not just black people, but immigrants from all countries and cultural backgrounds.

Not only was the locale of the Renaissance significant to the movement, but also was the term "renaissance." The term renaissance is defined as a re-awakening, re-birth, and re-defining period. Historical depictions and perceptions associated with African slaves and their arrival to America, descendants of those enslaved were in desperate need of a "re-awakening, re-birth, and re-defining" period of introspection and retrospection.

Without deducing or compartmentalizing the contributions of the Harlem Renaissance, one would venture to say those influential people who created the Harlem Renaissance, during the 1920s, have an intergenerational relationship with those influential people who are credited with starting the Hip Hop Movement, during the early 1970s, in New York. The connection between the Harlem Renaissance and Hip Hop culture could be

summarized using six descriptive categorizations:

1) The Klu Klux Klan's potential eradication of a
   Renaissance.
2) The controversial patrons of the Harlem Renaissance.
3) Old school Harlem Renaissance leaders driven by
   education and cultural progression.
4) Hustlers' ambitions begin to emerge during the Harlem
   Renaissance.
5) New school Harlem Renaissance leaders.
6) Musical geniuses, club scenes, and trendsetters.

The Klu Klux Klan Almost Single-Handedly Eradicated an
Essential Renaissance

The Harlem Renaissance did not begin during an idyllic

period in American history. Even though slavery was abolished in

1865, the mindsets and attitudes of many White people

(specifically those who lived in the south) were not embracive or respectful of the political decision to free slaves or make any descendant of slavery equal in the eyes of the law. Any movement that seeks to have a significant impact in history; especially a post-slavery period, struggled to gain a following, because American society was at war with itself.

In fact, if one were to look at the historical progression of descendants of slaves, a direct connection can be seen with the political group called the Klu Klux Klan (aka KKK). Historically, every time there appears to be a political progression for people of color (specifically those categorized as descendants of slavery), a new chapter of the KKK coincidentally would emerge. The goal of the KKK was to promote white supremacy, resist any attempts of change, and implement methods of intimidation, lynching, assassination, and exploitation. The most significant years for the KKK are 1866, 1915, and 1946 (Kneebone, 2012).

Examples in history show that after slaves were emancipated in 1865, six former confederates, in Pulaski, Tennessee, established the first chapter of the KKK in 1866 (Bryant, 2002). The initial group was considerable small and could be categorized as a social group; however, early on the group adapted the sheeted costumes (specifically the white outfits), violence, and fire burning practices to create fear. The use of white sheets were strategically chosen by the Klansman because during slavery the overseers would ride around the plantation at night on a white horse dressed in all white or all black demanding obedience and evoking fear into slaves (Fry, 1977). The overseer would also verbally warn the slaves to remain in their shacked logged cabins after a certain time of night; otherwise, a monster ghost would punish them (Fry, 1977). As irrational as this may sound to today's reader, many slaves were superstitious and would often pass the stories of fear down to each generation (Fry, 1977).

When former slaves began to migrate to places like Chicago, Detroit, and New York, during the Great Migration of 1910, a second chapter of the Klu Lux Klan was established in 1915. The 1915 chapter of the Klu Klux Klan appears to have been the most influential chapter, because this chapter of the KKK had the highest numbers of members and financial benefactors nationwide. The second chapter of the KKK was more organized and directed hate to various groups, such as Negros, Jews, and Catholics. The second chapter of the KKK also created a standard uniform, which consisted of an all outfit that included white capped hood that covered members faces and long gowns. The group also evolved the level of intimidation by burning religious crosses, people's houses, and even people. Lastly, the second chapter Klu Klux Klan group began to spread throughout states like "Alabama, Colorado, Georgia, Indiana, Louisiana, Oklahoma, Oregon, and Texas" (Lay, 2005). Not only did the group spread locational, but the groups "included prominent government officials and police officers" who were members and supporters of the Klan's agenda and political views (Lay, 2005).

When movements like the Civil Rights peaked and began to gain more prominence in American society, during the 1950s, the third chapter of the Klu Klux Klan started in the mid-1950s. The third chapter of the KKK struggled to maintain popularity throughout America, but continued to resist equality and combat desegregation. Even though the third chapter was not as influential as the second chapter, the political views and racial hatred remained strong among members and supporters of the KKK; especially in southern states. The Klu Klux Klan's creation and development is essential information to know, because the

KKK's existence created more than just superstitions, but legitimate fear, and paranoia; especially regarding governmental officials and police officers. Trusting and believing the very people who were elected to protect and serve society based on the law has never been fully believable among the descendants of slavery.

Individuals, like Alain Locke and James Weldon Johnson, were inspired to start the Harlem Renaissance. However, anyone who tried to create change, reveal alternative perspectives of Negros, or inspire equality often risked their lives to do so; regardless of whether a person lived up north or down south. No Negro; regardless of location, was exempt or safe from the influence and harassment of the Klu Klux Klan. Many members and supporters of the Klan were unknown and un-identifiable due to the groups secrecy and uniforms that covered the members faces.

Movements created by Negros, during the reconstruction period, were often met with resistance and often eradicated due to fear before the movement could gain any momentum. Examples of such resistance and eradication was displayed on June 1, 1921, when an all-black financially independent neighborhood called, *The Black Wall Street*, located in Greenwood (Tulsa, Oklahoma) was fire bombed by multiple two-seater bi-plane trainers (Madigan, 2001). These trainers were used often by the American government for front-line reconnaissance and light bombers (Madigan, 2001). Realizing the bombing: included governmental resources, an innumerable amount of black casualties, the permanent destruction of financially lucrative businesses, and the desolation of town that was filled with self-made businesspersons was devastating and tragic. Having one's livelihood and hard work destroyed by Whites revealed how powerful this small town had truly become.

The Black Wall Street was built by Blacks for the empowerment of blacks. The townspeople operated and owned banks, maintained schools, homes, laundry shops, hospitals, restaurants, supermarkets, post offices, bus, horses, and airplanes. Unfortunately, after the bombing, a permanent distrust in the government for many people of color (specifically Blacks) developed; especially those in Greenwood, as the town was never rebuilt and the story removed from most history books. The Black Wall Street's rise of influence was powerful, because this all-black town was able to thrive, when larger society (specifically Whites) were struggling financially. The Black Wall Street did not just thrive over-night, but was a town that had been thriving since the early 1900s. In other words, once slavery was abolished, many former slaves settled in oil rich states like Oklahoma. Various research suggests the average dollar traveled within The Black Wall Street neighborhood 36 to 100 times, before leaving the community and the daily income for business owners range between 100 and 500 dollars (Hayslett, 1996).

The history of The Black Wall Street continues to be problematic because with each generation the true story becomes distorted and compromised to disassociate the American government. Most of today's researched stories, of the bombing, suggest a connection to a possible or alleged rape of a white woman, by a black man, in an elevator, on May 31, 1921 (Madigan, 2001). Allegedly, a black man rapped a white woman and fled to the Greenwood neighborhood, resulting in riots and the neighborhood being burned down (Madigan, 2001). Another researched story alludes to another incident involving a black man. Allegedly, this black man was seen having a gun in a particular all white town nearby. After being seen with the gun, the black man was then questioned by a white man who wanted the black man to relinquish the gun. The black man refused to relinquish the gun to the white man, which leading to the Black

man being chased in to the Black Wall Street neighborhood

causing the subsequent riots and destruction of the town.

Additional researched stories may also suggest the Klu Klux Klan

alongside returning veterans from World War I had harbored

negative emotions for the towns success for a while (Madigan,

2001). As a result, the groups feelings of rage and jealousy of the

all-black towns financial status and potential power caused the

two groups to plan a strategic attack on the neighborhood. The

attack/bombing was planned to take place on June 1, 1921

(Madigan, 2001). Participants would shoot any black person on

sight, while simultaneously throwing Molotov cocktails (aka a poor

man's bomb) into the businesses, schools, and homes. Allegedly,

members of the Klu Klux Klan and war veterans decimated The

Black Wall Street community beyond repair, by ransacking the town, looting any remaining goods, and killing any black person that resisted or survived the bombing.

Regardless of whether one believes the American government is not capable of such actions against their own country or The Black Wall Street's status and casualties have been exaggerated, please consider the following:

- Many people died because of the color of their skin and their financial stability.
- Multiple lynchings occurred and were apparently justified without consequence.
- Purposely altered documentation exists throughout history distorting any notions about what really happened.
- The American government supported inequality privately, while promoting equality publicly.

If the historical implications and effects of The Black Wall Street are irrelevant, then why was the ingenuity and destruction of this town's impact erased from American history? Also, consider how

the diminishment of the Black Wall Street's possibly influenced

any potential Renaissance that included only Black patrons and

artists. Because of the Klu Klux Klan's increased power and

influence, specifically during the 1900s, any possible ventures of

success or progress made by Blacks could be ruined or

destroyed. In other words, had the Black Wall Street not been

destroyed, who knows if the Renaissance would have occurred in

Tulsa instead of Harlem? Terrorism is not just an act of terror

from outside entities or organizations, but also exists within and

one's own country, state, and community.

Money is Power...The Controversial Patrons Who Funded the Harlem Renaissance

Creating, promoting, and sustaining any movement can be

filled with an array of complexities and challenges; especially if that movement seeks to change or inspire people. Additional struggles occur because those who support the movement often deal with opposition, rejection, restrictions, and discrimination. A potential movement may endure even more, if that movement sets a precedence and occurs during a historical period when racism, lynchings, Jim Crow laws, and inequality among races *does not* exist. What is even more troublesome is that a movement requires more than just physical support of people; a pre-requisite of financial support is needed to ensure the impact and longevity of a movement. In other words, money has an amazing ability to allow a movement to progress in spite of the resistance that appears to emerge. Even though, the Harlem Renaissance introduced a plethora of talented, powerful, and intellectual thinkers and artists of our time, many of these individuals would never have been introduced to the world had it not been for financial benefactors.

Thanks to the vision of Alain Locke and the organizational skills of Charles S. Johnson, the Civic Club Dinner on March 21, 1924 was a successful networking event that allowed for artists, writers, musicians, intellectual leaders, and financial benefactions to commingle. Key benefactors, such A'Lelia Walker, Charlotte Osgood Mason, and Carl Van Vetchen became not only financial contributors, but also endorsers and active participants in the creation, promotion, and sustainment of the Harlem Renaissance. Securing funding would allowed artists, musicians, and writers literary work to have access to people locally and internationally. However, as the saying goes, "More money, more problems." Financial benefactors are a great asset; especially when attempting to create a movement, promote literature, and cultivate talent. However, when one's vision relies on outside funding, risks can occur. In other words, the person with the money will always control the talented person without the money.

A'Lelia Walker, heiress to Madame CJ Walker's hair-care empire, was a benefactor of the Harlem Renaissance. A'Lelia did more than just inherit her mother's empire; she actually helped sustain the business by opening stores throughout the United States and eventually opening a cosmetology school and salon in New York (Bundles, 2003). A'Lelia Walker's business savviness, some would say, was secondary to her party-hosting status. A'Lelia Walker was known as T*he Grand Dame of Harlem* and would have parties at her salons, as well as at her multiple million-dollar residences. The parties often served business and networking purposes, but were primarily done for celebratory purposes and entertaining other patrons, artists, writers, and intellectual thinkers. Walker's parties were legendary and often held theme parties that required guests to dress up accordingly. Like the other benefactors of the Harlem Renaissance, A'Lelia, was not exempt from controversy. At one A'Lelia Walker's party, she had all of her guest dress up to replicate life during slavery. Therefore, all white guests were required to wear tattered clothes, drink bath tub gin, and eat chitterlings in one section of her mansion, while all black guests dressed in tuxedos and gowns, drunk the finest of wines, dined in a lap of luxury eating lobster and various delicatessens (Watson, 1995, p.144).

As the saying goes, "One generation saves and the other generation spends." All of the parties, financing, and generosity that A'Lelia provided to others, in addition to the money she spent on outfits, she did not save any money for a rainy day. Unfortunately, when the Great Depression occurred, the hair-care empire began to decline. A'Lelia did not save enough money from her investments to sustain the financial decline. The effects of the Great Depression caused A'Lelia to auction off many of her most valuable possessions and residences (Bundles, 2003).

Another essential benefactor to the Harlem Renaissance was a woman named Charlotte Osgood Mason. Mason invested over 100,000 dollars (totaling about 2,000,000 dollars, in today's times) to Harlem Renaissance artists, writers, and intellectual thinkers (Matthias, 1923). Anyone who benefited from Mason's financial investments were required to call her "Godmother." Charlotte Osgood Mason's investment allowed for artists and writers like Alain Locke, Langston Hughes, Aaron Douglas, and Zora Neale Hurston to publish, promote, and become profitable. As great as her financial gifts were to the movement, writers, and artists, Charlotte Mason was authoritative and manipulative. Mason would approve, delay, or prevent the publication of books or art from being published, if the work did not meet her standards. Many beneficiaries of Mason's financial investment had mixed feelings about entering into a business partnership with Mason. Either you do what "Godmother" says or you lose your financial benefits.

The last pivotal benefactor of the Harlem Renaissance was a man named Carl Van Vetchen. Vetchen was not just a benefactor, but an actually participant (artist and writer) in the movement. Vetchen embraced and adored Negro people, the writings, and the art. Unfortunately, just like Mason, Carl Van Vetchen, would eventually be inclined to publish his own works, which included books, movies, and portrait photography reflective of the life and experiences of Negros in Harlem. In 1926, Carl Van Vetchen released a book called *Nigger Heaven,* which he described as a Harlemites paradise full of parties, music, drugs, sex, and a bevy of indulgences. Carl Van Vetchen claimed the book was a tribute to the Harlem experience and the title was to be complimentary; not offensive.

Despite Vetchen's explanation for choosing the controversial title for his book, the term, *Nigger Heaven*, has no positive connotation or historical empowerment. *Nigger Heaven* has two distinct meanings: The first meaning for *Nigger Heaven* pertains to the balcony of the church where only blacks sat. The second meaning for *Nigger Heaven* pertains to the idea that heaven is all-white and segregated. The release of Carl Van Vetchen's book caused controversy and raised questions, not just among critics, but participants and supporters. Older generations (DuBois and Washington) of the Harlem Renaissance wondered why Vetchen would release a book knowing the history surrounding the term nigger heaven. Was Van Vetchen that insensitive or self-absorbed to capitalize off such a horrific experience of slaves? While mostly older generations questioned Carl Van Vetchen's motives, the younger generations (Langston Hughes) of the Harlem Renaissance came to Vetchen's defense;

justifying his title's choice. No matter which stance one may take on such a controversial book title, both generations (old and young) had to wonder whether Carl Van Vetchen's decision helped or hurt the movement and race relations.

In other words, if white people are using the word "nigger," even in writing, a tension must be reconciled to avoid any questions of subliminal, subtle, or invisible racism. In addition, if white people are now writing black literature and producing black movies or plays, then the potential visibility of black authors and writers may become limited. People are more likely to buy a book about Negro culture from a white author than from a black author. Other issues like ghostwriting, plagiarism, and missing royalties would begin to emerge as well during the Renaissance, due to the influx of some White and Jewish patrons wanting to become active participants in the movement and usurp control and delivery of material because of financial investments in the movement, the artistry, and artists.

Regardless of the intentions of the three patrons (Walker, Mason, and Vetchen) mentioned and those not mentioned, the Harlem Renaissance was more than just a *New Negro Movement.* The movement could not have existed without patrons; specifically White and Jewish patrons. Therefore, the movement cannot be strictly defined as a "Negro Only" inspired movement, like that of The Black Wall Street. However, one would venture to say that the Harlem Renaissance was sustained, promoted, and documented historically better in comparison to The Black Wall Street, probably because the movement was inclusive to Whites and Jews and not exclusive to Negros only.

Old School Leaders Driven by Education and Cultural Progression

Old school simplistically is a term typically used in Hip Hop culture to define aspects of current culture that existed before one's generation. Those things that were once considered new, in style, current, or up to date will eventually be considered old school to a new and younger generation. In fact, the terms hip and hop could be historically connected to the Harlem Renaissance era. The word "hip," during the Harlem Renaissance era meant: cool, down, and knowledgeable. While the word "hop" meant: dance and movement. Ironically, placing these two terms together creates a movement that is birthed on being cool, down, and knowledgeable, while simultaneously incorporating elements of dance and movement. Throughout Hip Hop culture's history, each of these aspects defined by the terms hip and hop have been displayed and popularized repeatedly within each generation.

Like each generation, during the Harlem Renaissance, there were many leaders and visionary strategies dedicated to cultivating a level of awareness that ascribed to re-awaken the Negroes (freed and newly freed) consciousness. The process of awareness also included a need to re-define what it means to be a Negro in America, and encouraging Negroes to be re-born anew. There are many leaders and activists that helped propel this newfound awareness. However, for the sake of discussion, only a few distinct people will be strategically mentioned. Two distinct leaders that have poignantly promoted two distinct paths of progression, during the Harlem Renaissance, are W.E.B. DuBois (William Edward Burghardt DuBois) and Booker T. Washington. These two leaders (DuBois and Washington) provided, in short, two distinct strategies for the progression for everyone specifically the newly freed Negroes who were emancipated from slavery.

DuBois and Washington's paths for progression could be defined in many ways; however, an immediate description that comes to mind for DuBois' path is a book smart approach and Washington's path is a common sense approach. Both leaders would become advocates for cultural progression. Both leaders (DuBois and Washington) had distinct visions of progression for the New Negro, during the Harlem Renaissance era; regarding the progression and path of the New Negro, which often inspired some of most prolific literary debates. DuBois promoted the notion of a liberal arts education, encouraged a state of double consciousness, believed in change and equality through politics, and coined and purposed the Talented 10th. Washington promoted a trade school education, encouraged working with whites using a metaphor about fingers on a hand, and accepted upholding Jim Crow laws, while simultaneously endorsing self-sufficiency. Being book smart has many benefits, during the Harlem Renaissance, as well as now. Just as common sense is useful an essential trait for survival. However, having to decide whether to be book smart or exude common sense can be problematic; especially when inequality, racism, segregation, and limited opportunities for people of color specifically Negroes exist. The disagreement between these two prolific thinkers created a huge divide among the Negro audiences, because both paths of progression required different levels of patience and acceptance. In other words, one could either ascribe to change the world using one's intellect and political voice or change the world from the bottom-up (grassroots) through manual labor.

A liberal arts education, for DuBois, could offer the newly freed Negro an opportunity to learn beyond one's immediate experiences. Having a liberal arts education, allowed one to learn a little bit about everything politics, socialism, economics, philosophy, history, and more) for career diversity. In other words, if a Negro wanted to show one's value beyond stereotypical characteristics or caricatures based on singing and dancing, gaining a level of knowledge would suffice. DuBois believed that becoming knowledgeable about a bevy of topics historically, currently, and futuristically relevant creates an awareness that makes one indispensable and invaluable not just professionally, but personally. In addition to becoming marketable professionally, DuBois suggested that Negroes also learn how to develop a double consciousness. Exuding double consciousness is not to be confused with hiding one's true self or being a hypocrite (two-faced). Double consciousness, for DuBois, was an important technique that allowed the Negro to co-exist with whites and the white supremacy power structure without compromising one's personal goals and aspirations for change.

In other words, a double consciousness is what DuBois describes as the awareness of the *two-ness;* being an American and an African American (DuBois, 1903).

In order to survive and thrive, during the Harlem Renaissance, DuBois believed that all Negroes should operate with a double consciousness and maintain a constant awareness of being a direct descendant of slaves and navigating in a post-slavery era. Because of this double conscious awareness, one would have to constantly deal with having two inescapable thought processes: 1) being black 2) being black in a white world. How can one (specifically the newly freed Negro) be loyal to one's self, culture, and community, while at the same time being aware of the complexities of race, in the midst of trying to achieve levels of success, which include power, prestige, affluence, and influence. DuBois (1903) states:

It is a peculiar sensation, this double-consciousness, this sense of always looking at one's self through the eyes of others, of measuring one's soul by the tape of a world that looks on in amused contempt and pity. One ever feels his two-ness— an American, a Negro; two souls, two thoughts, two unreconciled strivings; two warring ideals in one dark body, whose dogged strength alone keeps it from being torn asunder (*Souls of Black Folk*).

In addition to the encouraging a liberal arts education and double consciousness, DuBois also was an advocate of change through politics. Just because slavery was abolished and a societal reconstruction period was beginning, DuBois realized that the current laws still promoted slave and slave master culture.

Laws, like the Jim Crow law, allowed segregation to exist without consequence, which, according to DuBois, "often enforced lynching and criminality without trials for white offenders; especially throughout the south. [Therefore], DuBois gradually concluded that only direct political agitation and protest could advance African American civil rights (DuBois, 1891)." Politics was an important area for the Negro, according to DuBois,

because the changes that needed to occur, regarding laws,

equality, and opportunity could only take place through the ability

to vote. Now that slavery had ended, DuBois asserted that "slave

codes," which were implemented to limit any resistance during the

slave era had now been strategically replaced with new codes.

"Black codes" were codes developed politically that:

> Penalized African Americans for offenses such as
> vagrancy and prevented them from testifying against
> White Americans, serving on juries, and voting. These
> disparate laws were then enforced by criminal justice
> practitioners such as police. Violators were often tried in
> court by all-White juries, found guilty, and punished by
> being made to work in the convict-leasing system (DuBois,
> 1901).

Because and promotion of the new codes being established,

during the post slave era, DuBois realized the importance of creating and partaking in movements like the N.A.A.C.P. (acronym means: National. Association for the. Advancement of. Colored. People.). Voting rights, for DuBois, allowed an opportunity for Negroes to create change on a local level, but also throughout the United States government.

DuBois' final concept for consideration, regarding the path of progression, was called the Talented 10th. The Talented 10th became a viable solution for creating and establishing sustainable Negro society through interrelationships. DuBois believed that "one in ten black men [should become] leaders of their race in the world, through methods such as continuing their education, writing books, or becoming directly involved in social change. He strongly believed that blacks needed a [higher] education to be able to reach their full potential (DuBois, 1903)."

DuBois' path of progression was thought to be selfishly exclusive, by some, and not coherently inclusive to everyone.

DuBois believed that only a selective group of talented individuals; specifically 10% of the Negro population would acquire enough power, affluence, influence, and success to save or redeem the remaining 90% of the Negro population; a population that would always be marginalized. Because of the lifetime marginalization that would be endured by 90% of the Negro population, the 90% Negro population culture's success would be contingent on the Talented 10th (the elite). The Talented 10th would be responsible for investing and empowering the other 90% of people achieve optimal success. DuBois' suggested solution created controversy among those belonging to the perceived 10 and 90 percent.

Some of those individuals, who DuBois would categorized as the Talented 10th, did not believe their position or status (financially, professionally, personally, communally, or politically) was established for the sole purpose of benefiting others without any immediate guarantee or reward for themselves. In other words, those individuals, who DuBois considered the Talented 10th, struggled with being automatically volunteered to help the remaining 90% of people obtain various levels of success; even if some of those people belonging to the 90% did not intend to become better or successful legally. Ironically, some of those individuals, who DuBois considered the 90%, struggle with being automatically deemed financially, professionally, personally, communally, or politically indigent. The perception, suggested by DuBois, that the 90% could never reach a level of elitism, in addition to obtaining any kind of notable success without the influence and affluence of Talented 10th was offensive and hopelessly limiting. DuBois's path of progression was starkly centered on acquiring awareness through education; hence the categorization of DuBois' path of progression as a book smart approach. W.E.B. DuBois' suggestions did not come without contempt and criticism; specifically from Booker T. Washington. Washington's approach was contrary to W.E.B. DuBois' book smart approach and focused more on self-sufficiency rather than dependency.

Booker T. Washington had a similar compassion and consideration for Negroes that extended beyond formal education. Washington's path of progression included a trade school education, encouraged working with whites using a metaphor about fingers on a hand, accepted upholding Jim Crow laws, and promoting endorsed self-sufficiency. Being book smart was as beneficial, during the Harlem Renaissance, as it is now. However, determining whether to pursue a higher education or exude a common sense approach can seem problematic in the midst of inequality, racism, segregation, and limited opportunities for people of color specifically Negroes exist.

For Booker T. Washington, a trade school education, which focused primarily on uniting the races through manual labor and using one's hands to provide financial stability for Negroes was more ideal, during the Harlem Renaissance. Booker T. Washington believed that a formal education was not an obtainable or beneficial goal, given the immediate needs of recently emancipated slaves. Cultivating a liberal arts education, for Washington, was a luxury that was not afforded to the masses; specifically ex-slaves whose primary skill included picking cotton. Pursuing a liberal arts education would not create an immediate impact financially, politically, professionally, or otherwise for Negroes, because the entire process of DuBois vision takes time to come to fruition.

For Washington lessons in the classroom about books, politics, business, religion, or arts had no immediate benefits in the daily lives of Negroes individually and collectively. In addition,

Washington believed that pursuing a liberal arts degree was not feasible because a huge percentage of ex-slaves were unable to read or write. Therefore, sending illiterate individuals to college was nonsensical to Washington. Success for, Washington, is best accessible familiarity. Washington believed that through familiarity financial success and stability could be achieved for the New Negro. For Washington, financial lucrative solutions rooted in manual labor, should be the primary goal for Negroes (especially newly freed slaves).

As a result, Washington's approach could be described as a common sense approach, because of the focus on immediate opportunities. Washington believed that a trade school education that promoted a vocational curriculum (which focused on becoming a carpenter, blacksmith, technician, or other vocations) created immediate opportune success as opposed to a liberal arts curriculum that created employment formidability. For

Washington, a trade school education made the most sense because many duties and requirements needed for a successful career in trade were already naturally cultivated and mastered by slaves for centuries during slavery. In addition, the potential apprenticeships given to those who obtained and participated in vocational studies would allow for immediate financial benefits and employment opportunities. Washington believed that if newly freed slaves joined the workforce (specifically manual labor), unity among races through work could occur.

Booker T. Washington often spoke about the need for racial unity through employment, regardless of current society's racial tension and segregation issues. Washington believed that white people were not the opposition, but part of the solution through partnership. Washington stated, in the 1895, *Atlanta Exposition Speech*, "In all things that are purely social we can be separate as the fingers, yet one as the hand in all things essential to mutual progress." Washington's approach to unity focused on solidifying working relationships with White people privately rather than publically denouncing White people for harsh crimes like lynchings, segregation, and Jim Crow laws. For Washington, rather than focus on the differences constantly expressed between the races, one should realize that a hand is still one entity in spite of the fingers being separate. In other words, segregation is not the as devastating as some may think (specifically DuBois) as long as the common goals being fulfilled are mutually beneficial. For example, Washington understood that white factory owners would need workers in industrial factories.

For Booker T. Washington, self-sufficiency was best fulfilled through proficiency, not invention. In other words, newly freed Negroes, from slavery, would have a better chance of survival by doing what was familiar; manual labor. For

Washington, manual labor skills were inherent to African slaves, because every day for centuries African slaves spent centuries picking cotton, overseeing plantation, agriculture, and tasks for centuries. Therefore, the sensible solution for the newly freed Negro to achieve any level of immediate success would be to obtain employment opportunities with manufacturing companies. Washington's' emphasis and suggestion was well received and accepted by White people; specifically those who were in support of Jim Crow laws. However, Washington's approach was not without criticism; especially from DuBois.

Ironically, both W.E.B. DuBois and Booker T. Washington believed that their independent visions and progressive strategies were the best option for the New Negro. DuBois' vision was in constant opposition of Washington's vision. Both leaders often engaged in a literary argument about one another's visionary approaches, intentions, and apparent self-aggrandizement. For example, DuBois allegedly referred to Washington as a *great accommodator*, because Washington appeared to accommodate anyone with money. In addition, Washington complied with segregation practices in his famous *Atlanta Exposition Speech*, while simultaneously remaining an active member of the Republican Party until his death (Gilmore, 2010, p. 20). However, Washington often described DuBois and his approach as bourgeoisie and elitist. Washington felt that DuBois' solution was not relevant or viable to a group of individuals that have come from a culture that had been berated, degraded, and forbidden to read and write.

Booker T. Washington believed that those who were newly freed were ill equipped to enter into higher education, when their previous experiences never cultivated higher education. Sitting in a classroom has potential future benefits, but not immediate benefits, which was what Washington believed the newly freed

Negro needed. Whether one agrees or prefers DuBois vision of progression over Washington's has personal significance; however, the most relevant part of is how DuBois and Washington's suggestions can be currently identified in society. Is higher education always the best method for progression and success or is cultivating a trade? Higher education versus a trade school education is a continual debate, not just during the early 1900s, but also today.

Interestingly enough, DuBois and Washington may not have agreed on their respective approaches for the New Negro. However, both men realized that neither vision could occur without financial patrons (educationally or industrially). Therefore, imagine what is a feasible solution for a person who has only known slavery, racism, prejudice, hate, death, and struggle. Imagine this same person working free without any financial stability, lacking any physically substantial benefits to show, and unable to obtain a proper education to obtain a long-term lucrative job. What would you do, if you were this person? Would you attend a school to become book smart without having money to survive in the mean time? On the other hand, would you do what makes common sense? Or, would you continue to work manually intense jobs that may have positional limitations; causing one to live paycheck-to-paycheck without any hope in ever getting a promotion? For some of the descendants of slavery who were newly emancipated; especially from the south, neither DuBois (book smart) nor Washington's vision (common sense) was feasible or considerate of the immediate need for money to survive; specifically those who migrated from southern states to Harlem, New York.

The Hustlers' Ambitions Emerges During the Harlem Renaissance

Aside from embracing the paths of progression (book and common sense smart) promoted by W.E.B. DuBois and Booker T. Washington, there was a third option for progressive success called *street smart*. The attributes and characteristics of what it means to be *street smart* can be defined differently depending on who defines the term. However, for the purposes of the discussion in this text, one would venture to say that being *street smart* involves a series of first-hand life experiences that has taught survival techniques (legal and illegal) that are not necessarily privy to those who possess book smart or common sense knowledge. In other words, street-smart individuals are students of some of life's harshest experiences; but smart enough to use those experiences to gain unpredicted success. During the Harlem Renaissance, many street-smart individuals emerged alongside some of the great leaders like W.E.B. DuBois and Booker T. Washington.

The term hustling, which includes legal and illegal activities, is an embedded part of Hip Hop's culture's psychology. In other words, having access to the trinity (money, power, and respect) has always been a primary goal of a culture that was barred from such influences, in America, initially. Hip Hop culture aspires and promotes this mentality; however, many people of all different racial, religious, and cross-cultural boundaries understand the significance of hustling. The term "hustling" is not exclusive to Hip Hop culture, but is inclusive to humanity as a whole. How one chooses to hustle, the purpose of the hustle, the length of time one hustles, and the methodical approach to hustling depends on the individual. As the saying goes, "The game does not change, only the players," remains true. Therefore, one should not be surprised to know or learn how impactful the hustlers of the Harlem were to an important movement like the Harlem Renaissance. Hustling is not exclusive to one state, one ethnic group, or one part of the world; however, for the sake of this book, the focus of hustling has been isolated to some of the *street smart* hustlers who directly influenced the Harlem Renaissance.

Some of these *street smart* hustlers of Harlem operated storefront businesses and clubs, while also promoting pimping and prostitutions, and engaging in bootlegging alcohol. The art of hustling knows no boundaries or limitations, which is why some of the most notorious gangsters throughout history dabbled in an array of illegal activities and businesses. In addition, it is important to note that these influential gangster who organized crime in Harlem inspired gangsterism and were mostly immigrants.

Money has always been an important component in starting and sustaining movements; especially movements of change. The Harlem Renaissance required patrons to support the purpose and agendas of the movement, which is the infamous Civic Club Dinner or March 21, 1924, included not only White and Jewish patrons, but gangsters as well. When seeking investors for a visionary movement, sometimes considering who contributes money or whether the money invested is from legal or illegal means is not as important as the movement's inception. For example, have you ever thought about how many people, who come from poverty to success, often have relational ties with hustlers (most of whom make their money illegally)? In other words, most hustlers; especially those hustlers who lived and thrived during the Harlem Renaissance, realized the value in recognizing talent and personal benefits.

Gangsters, during the Harlem Renaissance were smarter than people could imagine. In fact, one could go so far as to say that gangsterism, during the Harlem Renaissance, was even more appealing than DuBois and Washington's visions for progression. Entering a life of criminality seemed ideal and appealing; especially for some people who lived in poverty. Aspirations to become a gangster created and cultivated a generation and culture of *street smart* individuals, as opposed to the "book smart and common sense smart" approaches to success encouraged by W.E.B. DuBois and Booker T. Washington.

What is a hustler? How would you define a hustler? Who do you envision when you think about hustling? Do you believe there is a purpose in hustling? Can anyone become a hustler? These just a few questions are being raised, because the art of hustling is more than just the money one makes. Hustling is an old tradition that has been beneficial for some and consequential for others. During the Harlem Renaissance, hustlers began to emerge, because not everyone was educated enough to obtain a liberal arts degree (W.E.B DuBois' vision) or willing to work in factories (Booker T. Washington's vision) where managerial positions could never be obtained. What made matters worse is that many of the people who migrated from the south to New York struggled to make enough money because the rent was expensive. Many people wanted to succeed by obtaining a legal profession; however, those who participated in illegal activities were mostly hustlers. Imagine going to school to better one's future only to realize that the present day struggles do not wait for the future. Imagine taking a job at a factory, only to learn that one's employment status will never move upward. Hopelessness can cause the best of people to think alternatively and consider a life of crime, rather than one of lawfulness. In fact, hustlers, like

Father Divine, exploited many Harlem residents lack of hopelessness and offered hope.

Father Divine was known as a charismatic spiritual leader from the south who prophesied himself to be God (Melton, 1965). What makes the legend of Father Divine even more interesting is that there is no definitive history of Father Divines birth, birth name, or birthplace. In spite of the controversy surrounding his prophetic proclamation and his origin of birth, Divine promoted faith healing, economic independence, anti-lynching, and racial equality (Melton, 1965). Father Divine founded the International Peace Mission Movement and around 1920, Divine and his followers moved to an affluent all-white neighborhood in Sayville, Long Island, New York (Koehlinger, 2013). Father Divine appeared confident, spiritually influential, often wore expensive clothes, and drove a Cadillac; all of which infuriated his white neighbors (Koehlinger, 2013). Eventually, Father Divine moved his religious movement to Harlem, New York amidst the Great Depression. However, before he moved to Harlem, his reputation preceded him. Father Divine was known to take care of his followers and non-followers who were impoverished. When the Great Depression occurred, Father Divine accumulated a savings of 15 million in assets, which included business properties, homes, and possibly an island (Koehlinger, 2013). Father Divine's spiritual influence extended beyond the Negro population and included multi-cultural followers. In spite of Father's Divine affluence and influence, many people believed that Father Divine was nothing more than a hustler. Critics of Father Divine categorized him as nothing more than a "bootleg preacher" who was only concerned about money and power. For many people, the best options for immediate financial stability derives from hustling. Hustlers, during the Harlem Renaissance, rarely conducted legal business practices, but often dabbled in various illegal activities to acquire money. Some of these illegal activities included drugs, bootlegging alcohol (during the Prohibition), speakeasies, prostitution, pimping, bootleg preaching, numbers running, murderous activities, and gangsterism.

During the Harlem Renaissance, most gangsters engaged in a majority of illegal business practices. Casper Holstein (aka Bolito King) was born and raised in St. Croix, Virgin Islands. Holstein's upbringing would include a variety of experiences from being enlisted in the Navy to working on WallStreet, in New York. He would become a self-made man and creator of the numbers game, in Harlem, which would later become known as the lottery. The controversial numbers game, in short, was an illegal gambling game wherein bettors would choose a random three-digit number day-to-day with hopes of winning the lottery on the following day. The betting process was organized by having policy shop, where people could place bets, as well as number runners; mostly young males, who collected customers lottery picks and money. The policy shops, which included local businesses, such as barbershops, bars, pool halls, ice cream parlors, restaurants, and even churches allowed for the illegal gambling to go un-interrupted. Determining daily winners was the most controversial part of the game. Rumor has it the winning numbers were chosen sometimes based on the last three-digits of the local racetrack bets printed in the next day's newspaper or journal. Other times, the winning numbers would be based on clearinghouse numbers, sports scores, stock numbers, the total amount of money collected by number runners for the day, or a combination of all these factors. Casper Holstein's ability to promote and maintain such a lucrative business in Harlem was innovative.

Even though Casper Holstein was a leader in establishing the numbers game, Stephanie St. Clair(e) (aka Queenie) evolved the hustle into a thriving business that would help her create more business ventures throughout Harlem; eventually becoming the "Queen of Harlem." The birth origins of Stephanie St. Clair(e) are inconsistent. Some historians suggest that she was born in Martinique around 1886, while others acknowledge her birthplace as Marseilles, France or Guadalupe Island (Afryea, 2014). Regardless of the discrepancies surrounding her birthplace and age, documentation suggests Stephanie St. Clair(e) emigrated to Harlem, New York around 1912, penniless. St. Clair(e) was tri-lingual (spoke English, Spanish, French), cultured, educated, and fearless.

Stephanie "Queenie" St. Clair(e), like Holstein, was self-made. Queenie's influence; however, is more notable. Even though current day society has limited knowledge of her existence, Queenie's rise to power is monumental because she became the Queen of Harlem, amidst an array of male gangsters.

In other words, Stephanie St. Clair(e)'s level of affluence,

influence, and fearlessness was legendary in the streets of

Harlem ,during the Harlem Renaissance and influenced other

gangsters like Ellsworth "Bumpy" Johnson who was her right

hand, and future gangsters like Frank "King of Heroin" Lucas, who

was Johnson's right hand. What is even more shocking about St.

Clair(e) is that she was never intimidated by her male

counterparts and her reign of power was never compromised.

Not only was Stephanie St. Clair(e) the Queen of Harlem,

she was also wise enough to know that people are more likely to

respect and protect those gangsters who took care of their

communities. In other words, St. Clair(e) knew that if she took

care of the people of Harlem, the people of Harlem would take

care of her. Even though Stephanie St. Clair(e) ran several illegal

activities that made her money, she still made a point to give back

financially to the community (Afryea, 2014). To establish a positive rapport with the communities, Queenie would: give away

turkeys on Thanksgiving, Christmas gifts for Christmas, pay

doctor's bills and rent for people in the community, provide news

publications warning people against police corruption and police

brutality, and even became a patron to the Harlem Renaissance

by investing in the movement and the artists. Despite the means

that contributed to the successes of Casper Holstein and

Stephanie St. Clair(e), both "became rich enough to contribute to

philanthropic enterprises that helped better the community at

large, thereby sustaining the goal of self-determination that was

popular[ized]," during the Harlem Renaissance (Wintz and

Finkelman, p.921, 2004). Both individuals provided funding for

Harlem Renaissance movement, because both believed in

cultivating the art and talents of black culture.

Because of generous gifts to her customers, when deadly

wars, over running numbers, began to arise between Queenie

and the police, Luciano, and Schultz, people in the community protected her, fought with her against police corruption, and battled alongside her against her enemies. Queenie's financial gifts made it difficult for the police to arrest her and her enemies to murder her. Queenie was protected and loved by more people than she was hated because of her repeated acts of kindness and generosity.

Whether one agrees with a gangster's mentality and lifestyle of Harlem's is not the primary focus of this particular part of the book. However, the insight and reasons for what motivates a hustler is important. Often times, people assume that engaging in illegal activity was a first resort and not a last resort for establishing some level of financial stability, influence, and esteem. In other words, the lives of Harlem gangsters (specifically Holstein and St. Clair(e)) has fascinating influence on Hip Hop culture's obsession with money, power, and respect. Hip

Hop culture has embraced this notion of hustling and the bravado and lifestyles associated with Harlem gangsters like Holstein, St. Claire, Rothstein, Luciano, Schultz, Madden, Johnson, and so on. Therefore, one should not be surprised to see elements of gangsterism emerge in Hip Hop culture. However, one should be mindful that just because Hip Hop rappers endorse gangster imagery that does not mean that these artists are legitimate gangsters like those who lived, during eras like the Harlem Renaissance.

There is an unspoken truth that prostitution is the world's oldest profession. If this were true, then pimping would most likely be considered the second oldest profession. Sex has and will always make money; hence, the motto "Sex Sells." Because Harlem, during the 1920s, provided a smorgasbord of ways to make money, one should not be surprised to know that pimping was a viable option for making money; especially for those who were migrating from down south to the north, had no money, or education. Many of the gangsters listed, in this particular part of the book, owned businesses and clubs that catered to more than just dancing and entertainment for their customers. Because pimping and prostitution was illegal, and eventually alcohol, during the Prohibition, gangsters would use legitimate business locations as storefronts for illegal business activities, which often included drugs, sex, and alcohol. Interestingly enough, most of the patrons to New York's illegal activities included notable men; specifically political figures, gangsters, and police officers (Chepesiuk, 2013). The strategic business savviness of gangsters, during the Harlem Renaissance would provide a blueprint for future generations that aspired to become gangsters.

One respected principle of Hip Hop culture, initially, was authenticity. An artist's authenticity provided a level of realism to a rappers artistry, reflective of real life experiences, and was appreciated by audiences; especially those who were living the same experiences. When discussing the impact of gangsterism, knowing Hip Hop history becomes essential. West Philadelphia rapper, Schoolly D (birth name Jesse B. Weaver Jr.), is credited with being the first rapper to mention the word *gangster* on a rap song, in 1984 (Emery, 1997). The song was entitled *Gangster Boogie* talked about getting over on people, smoking jays (aka a joint or marijuana), and pulling out 8's (aka guns) (Emery, 1997). Schoolly D released another song in 1985 called *P.S.K., What Does It Mean?* The lyrics explained the acronym P.S.K., which means Park.Side.Killers. and boasts about weed, drinking, cocaine, sex, prostitution, and pistols. These two particular songs would become blueprints for the rap genre called gangster rap.

Even though Schoolly D is known as the first gangster rapper, in Hip Hop culture, the actual gangster rap genre did not become noticeably mainstream until the early 1990s, when West

Coast rappers like N.W.A. (Niggers. With. Attitudes) and Ice T

began to emerge. The connection and obsession with

gangsterism, in Hip Hop, was heavily influenced by the actual

gangsters. Rappers; especially those who emerged during and

after the early 1990s began to emulate and discuss gangster

activities in their lyrics, have affiliations with real gangsters, and

some rappers would even name themselves after real life

gangsters. Interestingly enough, Hip Hop culture in many ways

has become over-saturated with individuals who have attempted

to capitalize and monopolize the lifestyles of actual gangsters who

began to emerge, during and after the Harlem Renaissance. Rap

names like Capone, Noriega, Dillinger, Gotti, Machine Gun Kelly,

Escobar, Chief Keith (ironically mentioned in Schoolly D's

P.S.K...song), Frank White, 50 cent, "Freeway" Rick Ross (name

has been divided into two names Freeway or Rick Ross, have

become popularized since the invasion of gangster rap, in Hip Hop culture.

Even though gangsterism has been consistently embraced and endorsed by Hip Hop culture, the distinction between reality and fantasy has always been an important part of authenticating Hip Hop culture; specifically rap artists. For example, there is a vast difference between gangsta and gangster. Have you ever noticed the spelling in record stores? Often times in the stores and online the word is spelled g-a-n-g-s-t-a compared to how the word is spelled when discussing historical figures, which is g-a-n-g-s-t-e-r. The term "gangst(a)" that ends in the letter "a" is significant because those who often adopt this spelling are actors, whereas the term "gangste(r)" reflects those who have actually lived a life that included gangster activities. The letter "r" is significant because these are individuals who could be considered the real deal.

Realizing that gangsters, during the Harlem Renaissance, were part of organized crimes, committed mass atrocities, and orchestrated criminal transgressions reveals a level of authenticity that cannot be doubted or dismissed as fallacies, which is a contrast to the life experiences of a majority of today's rap artists. Most of today's rap artists claim a lifestyle for financial gain and entertainment purposes only, while never having lived or experienced the lyrics being rapped. Think about the individuals Harlem gangsters mentioned and how influential these gangsters' criminal enterprises were during the Harlem Renaissance. Many of the gangsters that emerged during the Harlem Renaissance, influenced current and future generations, cultural trends, and set standards of how to manage illegal business legally.

Hip Hop's origins were based on telling rhymes (stories) about real life first-hand and second-hand experiences. Hip Hop stories, like the stories of New York gangsters, range from inspiration to tragedy and includes experiences ranging from legal

success to illegal success through pimping and prostitution. The

entertainment value that some find with gangsterism, during the

Harlem Renaissance and even today is essential. Some of the

most vulgar imagery and lyrical content described in today's rap

songs still allow for some audiences to receive important lessons

about life, loyalty, trust, and business principles. As absurd as

this may sound, have you ever realized the business principles

associated with pimping? For example, the basic principles of

pimping includes three basic elements: a pimp (smooth talking,

alleged protector, and money collector), a ho (prostitution), and a

john (the customer). Simplistically, one should note that the john

(customer) employs the ho (prostitute) for sexual favors or

companionship. The ho (prostitute) is known to work day-and-

night for money. However, the ho (prostitute), willingly gives all

the money earned to person who is believed to have one's best interest at heart; the pimp (the smooth talking alleged protector). As vile and anti-respectful as pimping sounds to the average morally conscious citizen, the lessons of pimping are foundational principles of business; specifically the music business. Think about the average rap career. Who is the pimp, ho, and john in this scenario? The pimp represents the record label and adopts the same principles that a pimp on the street takes serving as a smooth talking, alleged protector, and money collector). The ho represents the rap artist who works hard for every dime made and gives the majority of the money earned back to the pimp. The john represents the consumers of rap who continue to pay money to be indulged and entertained by the ho (rap artist). What is important to know is that when a ho (rap artist) is good and gains enough of the pimps-record label trust, the ho (rap artist) will recruit other hoes (rap artists) for employment. Have you ever noticed when a rap artist gains a certain level of success, in the rap industry, that rap artist will often invest in a separate or newly founded label, which still remains affiliated with the primary label? What is even more interesting is that rap artists often sign close friends and family members to the newly formed label; starting the pimp, ho, john cycle all over again.

In addition to the business format of the music industry, additional controversy surrounds the lifestyles associated with gangst(a)s and gangste(r)s, essential principles of survival can be learned. Unfortunately, the current state of rap struggles between whether to maintain authenticity or just make money entertaining. Some of the inconsistencies may be based on an overindulgence of g-a-n-g-s-t-a-s and not g-a-n-g-s-t-e-r-s. Today's rap artists rarely tells *current* first-hand experiences, but rather describes attributes and second-hand accounts of a life never lived. Distinguishing between those who are real and those who are fake has and continues to a relevant topic of conversations, among critics and Hip Hop enthusiasts alike.

New School Harlem Renaissance Leaders

One of the most intriguing elements about the creation and sustainment of a movement are the people that come together to make a movement successful. Throughout this particular section of the book a variety of people from various economic statuses, professions (legal and illegal), ethnicities, and generations have come together with noble intentions to fulfill a vision of creating a Renaissance in Harlem, New York. What is even more interesting is that young people were included in the vision. In order for any movements' legacy to be sustained, young people must be included and encouraged to contribute. The Harlem Renaissance was no exception to this rule. In fact, the younger generation provided an alternatively relevant perspective compared to older generations (DuBois and Washington) perspective, which focused heavily on education. The alternative perspective to the Harlem Renaissance might not have existed had young people been excluded from the March 21, 1924 Civic Club Dinner.

There are a number of young people who made significant contributions to the Harlem Renaissance through literature, music, art, and playwrights. Writers like Countee Cullen, Langston Hughes, Zora Neale Hurston, Jean Toomer, Claude McKay, F.E. Miller, and Aubrey Lyles were inspired by their real life experiences, which often included an uncensored truth about personal experiences and life in Harlem. Before focusing on some of the individual works of the artists mentioned, one must note the initial message of the Harlem Renaissance often conflicted with the reality of life in Harlem, New York. The younger generation (Cullen, Hughes, Hurston, Toomer, McKay, and *Shuffle Along* playwrights Miller and Lyles) often felt inclined to combat one-sided notions that the New Negro had evolved beyond their unconscionable roots. Do you tell the unadulterated truth about being a Negro in America, while living in Harlem's light and darkness? On the other hand, do you censor the truth to promote a singular view of the New Negro, which was based on sophistication, educational success, and social, political, and economic awareness? In other words, do you write half of the story or the whole story, even if the movement is seeking to be re-defined, re-born, and re-awakened?

Writers like Countee Cullen managed to accumulate success in black and white circles, because of his educational path. Cullen was educated at primarily white universities and influenced by the teachings to the point that he strictly wrote with the intentions of promoting a sense of oneness, during the Harlem Renaissance. In other words, Countee Cullen was conscientious about writing material that seemed to promote only blackness.

Even though Cullen made significant contributions to the Harlem

Renaissance, he was not exempt from criticism; especially from

other young intellectual thinkers. Countee Cullen was a great

promoter of the older generation's agenda, which focused on the

educated Negro. Cullen also supported many of his youthful

counterparts (Hughes, Hurston, Toomer, McKay, and other

writers and artists); however, Cullen often:

> Prodded black writers to censor themselves by avoiding
> some things, some truths of Negro life and thought ... that
> all Negroes know, but take no pride in. Cullen went on to
> say that, showcasing unpleasant realities would [only]
> strengthen the bitterness of our enemies and thereby
> weaken the bridge of art between blacks and whites
> (Davis, 1974).

While members of his own generations felt simultaneously inspired and restricted by Cullen's critique of their work for potentially having a negative effect on race relations or labeling their work "too black." Cullen, when doing a review of Langston Hughes work, suggested that Hughes (who was the first poet to fuse poetry with jazz) cease combining his poetry with jazz, because continuing to do so could detract audiences from realizing the true power in his words.

Contrary to Countee Cullen's perception, Langston Hughes, Zora Neale Hurston, Jean Toomer, Claude McKay, playwrights Miller and Lyles, and other noteworthy young writers remained dedicated to promoting authenticity in their works. For example, *Shuffle Along (1921),* was the one of the premiere Negro musical theatre productions on Broadway, written by F.E. Miller and Aubrey Lyles (Negro writers) that featured an all-Negro cast of innovative and legendary writers, musicians, and actors.

The production of the play was a historical victory for the New

Negro. However, the musical for many critics included blackface

characters and perpetuated stereotypical perceptions about trust

and attractiveness surrounding dark-skinned, mulatto, and light-

skinned Negros. These sentiments were described in a song

sung at the end of the musical:

> A high brown gal
> Will make you break out of jail,
> A choc'late brown
> Will make a tadpole smack a whale,
> But a pretty seal-skin brown,
> I mean one long and tall,
> Would make the silent sphinx
> Out in the desert bawl,
> If you've never been vamped
> By a brown skin,
> You've never been vamped at all.

As monumental as the *Shuffle Along* musical was, some Negro intellectuals questioned whether the musical set a positive or negative standard of success, for musicals. In other words, would future musicals produced only do well if Minstrel Show elements like blackface and stereotypes were depicted?

In spite of the constructive criticism of some Negro intellectuals, regarding the musical *Shuffle Along*, the playwr, musicians, and actors continued to receive successful reviews. White and Negro audiences enjoyed the musical, which led to the production of additional musicals that included similar characters and stereotypes. F.E. Miller and Aubrey Lyles, in spite of the controversy, considered comedy; even stereotypical comedy, to be culturally relevant.

Other Harlem Renaissance writers like Langston Hughes, Zora Neale Hurston, Jean Toomer, and Claude McKay, shared F.E. Miller and Aubrey Lyles' cultural sentiments. Hughes,

Hurston, Toomer, and McKay were dedicated to revealing all sides of the Negro experience. The youthful authors were inspired to create a literary magazine called *Fire!!*, in 1926 (Johnson and Johnson, 1979). The magazine sought to focus on "edgy issues in the Black community, such as homosexuality, bisexuality, interracial relationships, [mulattos], prostitution, and color prejudice within the Black community" (Johnson and Johnson, 1979). Of course, these topics contrasted any notion of the intellectual and sophisticated image of the Negro, which was heavily promoted and endorsed by those literary thinkers who believed in positivity over negativity. However, the younger generational writers like Langston Hughes, believed in the importance of a magazine like *Fire!!*, in spite of the controversial content. Hughes expressed that the magazine name (*Fire!!*) was symbolic. The younger generation represented the new school of thought for the Harlem Renaissance and sought to:

Burn up a lot of the old, dead conventional Negro-white ideas of the past ... into a realization of the existence of the younger Negro writers and artists, and provide us with an outlet for publication not available in the limited pages of the small Negro magazines then existing (Samuels, 2000).

In other words, Hughes and his co-authors believed that the information and thoughts shared in the magazine were not just controversial entertainment for readers, but essential to the movements' authenticity. Ironically, the infamous *Fire!!* magazine would only print one publication. The magazine's name choice was prophetic beyond anyone's imagination. After the first issues was published, the magazine's publishing headquarters was burned down ending any potential future publications (Hutchinson, 2007).

History reveals that three things have been consistent throughout society; sex, drugs, and parties, similar to Rock-and-

Roll's motto. The Harlem Renaissance represented a level of educational and intellectual progress for current and future generations who are descendants of slaves. An important part of being emancipated from slavery was not just physical freedom, but freedom to express one's self without shame, fear, judgment, or reproach. Some poets sought to address racial issues, by reflecting on personal experiences, racism, and cultural history. Poems that signify such expression and conflictions are described in poems by Countee Cullen (*Incident* and *What Is Africa to Me?)* and Langston Hughes (*The Negro and The Racial Mountain*).

<u>Incident</u>
(By Countee Cullen)

Once riding in old Baltimore,
Heart-filled, head-filled with glee,
I saw a Baltimorean
Keep looking straight at me.

Now I was eight and very small,
And he was no whit-bigger,--
And so I smiled, but he poked out
His tongue and called me, "Nigger."

I saw the whole of Baltimore
From May until December;
Of all the things that happened there,
That's all that I remember.

The Negro Artist and the Racial Mountain

(By Langston Hughes)

We younger Negro artists who create now intend to express our
individual dark-skinned selves without fear or shame.
If white people are pleased we are glad. If they are not, it doesn't
matter. We know we are beautiful. And ugly, too. The tom-tom
cries and the tom-tom laughs. If colored people are pleased we
are glad. If they are not their displeasure doesn't matter either.
We will build our temples for tomorrow, strong as we know how,
and we will stand on top of the mountain, free within ourselves.

What is Africa to Me?

(By Countee Cullen)

What is Africa to me:

Copper Sun or scarlet sea,

Jungle star or jungle track

Strong bronze men or regal black

Women from whose loins I sprang

When the birds of Eden sang?

One three centuries removed

From the scenes his fathers loved,

Spicy grove, cinnamon tree,

What is Africa to me?

The ability to create work that is reflective of one's emotion and

experiences realistically was not just essential for the New

Negro's growth, but America's growth. Each of these poems

offered insight about perceptions. Perceptions regarding race, freedom, and cultural connections.

Musical geniuses, club scenes, trendsetters, and rent parties

If writers, artists, and playwrights narrated the Harlem Renaissance, then club scenes infused with jazz and blues musicians provided the soundtrack, while fashion trendsetters painted an inalienable picture of the full experience of Harlem. Fashion trends evolved, during the Harlem Renaissance, especially for Negro women. Because the Harlem Renaissance was a progressive movement, men and women's fashion trends evolved; especially when dressing to enjoy Harlem's nightlife. During the Harlem Renaissance, women's fashion was no longer relegated to just skirts, dresses, blouses, coats, shoes, and traditional accessories (Smith, 2011). Women were now rebelling against traditional clothing trends and wearing pants along with clothes that revealed one's neck, bust, and waist (Smith, 2011).

Women, during the Harlem Renaissance, also wore: pin-curled hairstyles, flamboyant jewelry, ball gowns, cocktail dresses, pearls, beaded necklaces, ankle strapped shoes, rhinestone clothing, cloche hats, animal furs, decorative headbands, and clothing popularized by flapper girls (Smith, 2011). Men styles evolved as well and included zoot suits, expensive and tailored suits with handkerchiefs, feathered hats, conk hairstyles, (pocket watches with the chain attached to one's pants (Smith, 2011).

Most of the jazz and blues musicians that emerged, during the Harlem Renaissance, were former Vaudeville actors. Jazz and blues are not exclusive to the state of New York, as New Orleans and Chicago had their own regional styles of the two musical genres. Typically, jazz focused heavily on instruments, while blues focused more on lyric content. Both genres (jazz and blues) are reflective of the call-and-response technique; a technique that derived during the days of slavery. During the 1920s, Harlem, New York's style of jazz and blues differed in sound from places like New Orleans and Chicago.

The jazz musicians of Harlem Renaissance was just as diverse as the cultures who migrated to Harlem, New York. Jazz musicians, during the Harlem Renaissance incorporated deliberate and improvisational syncopations. Artists like Louis "Satchmo" Armstrong. However, some artists like Chick Webb, Count Basie, Duke Ellington, and Cab Calloway, Fletcher Henderson, incorporated jazz with big bands, which aided in the big band phenomenon. Audiences enjoyed "the sound of jazz music, but not quite the format of the small group or (worse) soloist" (Scaruffi, 2007). The big bands of jazz offered a compromise: jazz music with improvising soloists and music produced at a loud enough sound quality for dancing. Another great thing about jazz is the evolutionary and improvisational side of the music, which allowed for other evolved into various forms of jazz like ragtime, swing jazz, and eventually be-bop. Artists like Ella Fitzgerald popularized scat singing, while artists like Jelly Roll Morton and Willie "The Lion" Smith, combined elements of jazz and blues to "create lyrics and beats that reflected the excitement of the time" (Ryan, 2005, p. 15).

Blues musicians, on the other hand, entertained audiences by sharing personal experiences. Blues music often provides a glimpse into one's life through the lens of hopelessness. In other words, blues lyrics often focused on complicated issues like drugs, relationship problems, life tragedies, sexuality, financial struggles, and distrust of people. Harlem artists like Gertrude "Ma Rainey" Pridgett, dubbed the Mother of Blues, provided audiences with hit songs like *Trust No Man* (1926) and *Prove It On Me* (1928) that revealed her authenticity, showmanship, and transparency (Lieb, 1983). Other notable blues, during the Harlem Renaissance, included artists like Bessie Smith, Ethel Waters, Adelaide Hall, and Mamie Smith. In spite of the drama and controversy surrounding blues music, most audiences appreciated the authenticity and honest vulnerability that artists showed while singing, which made the music transformative and relational.

The hottest clubs had the greatest acts, music, dances, and stylish trendsetters. Jazz and blues musicians had a profound effect on the Harlem Renaissance, because music has an amazing ability to bring people together. The Jungle Alley (cabaret district) was located between Lenox and Seventh Avenue's- 133rd street. Local Harlem residents coined the street's name, because the three of the top clubs (Smalls Paradise, Connie's Inn, and the Cotton Club) in Harlem, New York, were located in black neighborhoods (Watson, 1995).

Edwin Smalls became one of Harlem's most successful

Negro club owners. Smalls owned two popular clubs, during the

Harlem Renaissance: The Sugar Cane Club and Smalls Paradise.

The Sugar Cane Club, known as a lap joint, located on 135th and

Fifth Avenue, in 1917 (Watson, 1995). The club operated as a

cheap late-night speakeasy club that catered to a racially mixed

lower class crowd, even though only a few Whites could be found

at the club on any given day (Watson, 1995). The club was

popular, but would never be greater than the club's successor,

Smalls Paradise.

Smalls Paradise was owned by Edwin Smalls (a former

elevator operator) and was located on 2294 ½ Seventh Avenue,

near 135th Street. Smalls Paradise was a basement club that

catered to a racially and economically diverse clientele. Charlie

Johnson led the club's house band and the club's best nights of

operation were Sunday nights; followed by Monday morning

breakfast dances, which featured twenty-five to thirty dancers and two dozen musicians (Kellner, 1984). Famous musicians, writers, and artists patronized Smalls Paradise daily. Writer and photographer Carl Van Vetchen was one of the most loyal customers of Smalls Paradise. After Carl Van Vetchen's, 1926 book, *Nigger Heaven*, many people believed the book was based on Smalls Paradise (Wintz and Finkelman, 2004). Because of this belief and the offensive nature of the book, Carl Van Vetchen would be permanently banned from Smalls Paradise (Wintz and Finkelman, 2004). However, what insulted some Negroes entertained and intrigued White readers; making Vetchen's book a number one seller (Garber, 1983).

In spite of the loss of Van Vetchen's patronage, Smalls Paradise remained successful, even during the Great Depression. Interestingly, after the Harlem Renaissance ended, Smalls Paradise would hire notable waiters like Malcolm Little (later known as Malcolm X) and would eventually be purchased by basketball legend Wilt Chamberlain around the 1960s. Connie's Inn was another club located on Jungle Alley. Connie's Inn was located on 131st and 7th Avenue (Cullen, 2007). The club was owned and established, in 1923, by three German bootlegging brothers: Conrad (Connie) Immerman, George Immerman, and Louie Immerman (Cullen, 2007). Connie's Inn, like the Cotton Club, operated and served whites-only, but employed some of the world's most talented Negros. Connie's Inn was popular among white audiences; however, the club attracted the best and worst of Harlem. One newspaper, *The New York Age*, published by a Negro writer, exclaimed that the Immerman's club was opened to indulge white audiences with illicit and illegal gangster activities, which included cocaine, gambling, bootleggers, and rumrunners (The Young and Meyers, 2009).

In spite of the dangerous activities rumored to have occurred at Connie's Inn, some Harlemites attributed Connie's Inns' initial success to the clubs ideal location. The Connie's Inn coincidentally was located next to the Famous Tree of Hope (Young and Meyers, 2009). The Tree of Hope was large chestnut that many Harlemites believed had the power to give good fortune to those who rubbed it (Young and Meyers, 2009). Ironically, after the Apollo Theater was renovated from a burlesque venue, in 1935 by Frank Schiffman and Leo Brecher to a talent show venue to search for new Negro talent and promote Negro performers. Talent show performers rubbed a piece of the Tree of Hope, which is now in the form of a tree stump, for good luck before going on stage to compete in the talent show competition at the Apollo Theatre's. Prior to the Great Depression, Connie's Inn enjoyed some prosperous and enjoyable years, before closing. Connie's Inn, during the Harlem Renaissance, had become a suitable rival to the Cotton Club for white audiences.

During the Harlem Renaissance, the world-renowned Cotton Club (formerly called Club Deluxe) was elite among other clubs. The Cotton Club was owned by Owney "The Killer" Madden. The club was the most popular whites-only venue, during the Harlem Renaissance, and constantly "reproduced the racist imagery of the times, often depicting blacks as savages in exotic jungles or as darkies" on a southern plantation (Watson, 1995). Under Madden, the Cotton Club had a strict code of employees. Female dancers at the Cotton Club were held to strict standards; "they had to be at least 5'6" tall, light skinned with only a slight tan, and under twenty-one years of age" (Watson, 1995). Dancers, performers, and waiters were hired solely to cater and entertain white audiences and were not allowed to eat or drink with or among white customers. No matter how entertained the white audience was at the Cotton Club, "the division between the performers and the audience was more carefully maintained than in any other club in Harlem" (Watson, 1995).

The Savoy Club was owned by Jay Faggen and a Jewish mobster named Moe Gale (Stern, 2012) opened on March 12, 1926. The Savoy Club, differed from the Cotton Club, in that the Savoy promoted a no discrimination policy and accepted a multi-racial community of artists and audiences. The Savoy Club would immediately become known as the "Home of Happy Feet," because people danced non-stop at the club during the weekdays, not just on the weekends (Stern, 2012). The club also served as a location for dance competitions and the popularization of dance trends, like the Lindy Hop, Charleston, the Shim-Sham Shimmy, the revival of the Cakewalk, American Tango, Boogie-Woogie, Black-Bottom, the Snake hips, and Swing dancing (Wintz and Finkelman, 2004). The Savoy was unique because the club also had a comedy club attached to the venue, called the Vaudeville Comedy Club. The Vaudeville Comedy Club, when not in use primarily for comedy, served as a private after-hours club for blacks-only (exclusive to performers and friends of the performers only) located in the basement of the Savoy Club.

Even though segregation existed, during the Harlem Renaissance, the excitement and enjoyment of Harlem's nightlife was a commonality shared among all people, regardless of whether or not one partied at whites-only club or an integrated club. Harlem's nightlife offered any and every one an opportunity to indulge freely in one's fantasy, in spite of the ongoing realities of segregation, racism, and inequality. As talented and famous as some artists, musicians, actors, and dancers were, many still were not allowed to rent certain properties, because of their ethnicity. Not only was one's skin color an important factor in segregation, but also classism. Most apartments that were rented, during the Harlem Renaissance, were expensive, because people (Negros, Italians, Irish, Latinos, and Jews) were migrating to Harlem constantly and landlords wanted to capitalize financially from the new migrants.

Unfortunately, not everyone in Harlem could live the glamourous life of rich and famous Harlemites. For example, during the height of the Harlem Renaissance, "the average Harlem resident spent 40 percent of his or her income on rent-and if it wasn't paid by Sunday the landlord put the furniture on the street on Monday morning" (Watson, 1995). The constant paranoia surrounding one's ability to pay the rent and a potential increase in rent did not allow some of the people to enjoy life outside of work. Because of high rent and a lack of money, many Harlemites could not afford to go to the clubs in their neighborhoods. Therefore, many Harlemites became creative and decided to party at home rather than try to get in a segregated club or a club that had limited space. Rent parties served two purposes: an ability to raise money for the rent and an ability to have fun without leaving home. Rent parties often included live or recorded music, food and drink for sale, and even space for those who wanted to have sex or gamble. Those who had a little more affluence would engage in a different kind of party known as buffet flats. Buffet flats were known as the parties where anything goes, including sexual fantasies (Garber, 1989). A lot of the top leaders, thinkers, and artists attended the parties and found inspiration for songs. These buffet flat parties often took place after hours in someone's apartment or mansion. A'Lelia Walker, Casca Bonds, and Alexander Gumby were a few people known to have thrown buffet flat parties (Watson, 1995).

Jazz, blues, club scenes, fashion trends, and rent parties, during the Harlem Renaissance were monumental to a holistic picture of life in Harlem, New York. The nightlife in Harlem inspired audiences to do more than just listen to music, but embrace all that this progressive movement had to offer. Harlem provided people with an opportunity to be re-awakened, re-born, and re-defined about the struggle and progress of a culture of people who were attempting to emerge from non-relevance to relevance and from illiterate to literary geniuses. "The rebirth of African American culture was composed of ingenious works of art, uplifting and eloquent poets, masterful musicians, inspirational political activists, creative painters, inventive sculptors, prolific thinking novelists, dramatic playwrights, visionary choreographers, natural actors, excellent journalists, and imaginative actors" (Black, 2006). Unfortunately, the Harlem Renaissance was short lived and the influence of the movement condensed to five years, because of an array of factors; ignited by the Great Depression of 1929.

United We Stand, Divided We Fall

Unfortunately, the Harlem Renaissance; specifically the literary and artistic side of the movement, began to decline, at the arrival of the Great Depression. The Great Depression started in 1929 and had an immediate effect on all Americans. The Great Depression affected a lot of people's ability to make money, pay bills, and eat; including rich people. The vivacious side of Harlem quickly became dull and depressing. Finding inspiration and entertainment became the primary focus for many people; especially Harlemites. Even though the Great Depression would be the primary event that caused the short-lived movement's demise, other signs that the Harlem Renaissance was entering a decline was ever-present. Initial signs of the Harlem

Renaissance's decline began with the literary side of the movement.

Since the creation of the movement, literature was a primary tool to offer the New Negro an opportunity to be re-awakened, re-born, and re-defined. Many readers; specifically, those belonging to the Negro population, appreciated the initial sentiments shared about the importance of Negros being education and enlightened. Unfortunately, after several publications began to print the same or similar content about the educated Negro, many people; especially the younger generation of Negros, dubbed the literary side of the movement boring. In other words, readers began to find the writings redundant and lacking any real life relevancy. These sentiments were not just shared by outsiders, but insiders associated with the Harlem Renaissance as well. Writers Langston Hughes, Zora Neale Hurston, and Claude McKay began to detach themselves from the movement, because only education and racially sensitive content was approved and supported.

Disagreements among people are a common part of history; especially regarding division among people within and outside of a particular culture. Understanding the impact of relational disagreements, during the Harlem Renaissance, are important to discuss because divisions can cause a vital movement to become stagnant, decline, or end. The Harlem Renaissance served as a "melting pot" for cultural diversity; however, divisions existed and had a profound impact on the lifespan of the Harlem Renaissance long-term. Key divisions included the following:

1) South versus North (Blues versus Spirituals)
2) Divisions Among the Visionaries (Patrons versus Artists)

3) Common Sense versus Book Smart versus Street Smart
4) Segregation in Harlem
5) Older Generation versus Younger Generation

South versus North (Blues versus Spirituals)

Have you ever felt isolated in a place where you believed you would be embraced? Have you ever tried to listen to a new genre or style of music only to end up reverting to familiar music that you know? These questions could seem frivolous to the average person, but these questions created an unfortunate division between northern Negros (those who already lived in Harlem, New York prior to the Great Migration) and southern Negros (those who migrated to Harlem, New York). Freedom, for a slave down south, was epitomized in notions of life in the north. The north represented a life free of slavery and all the struggles, stresses, fears, abuse, death, and paranoia experienced in the south. Spirituals, which were created by southern slaves, often reflected the ideal life up north by describing the geographical

location as heaven, freedom, a safe haven, or place of hope.

Surprisingly, living up north, for a newly freed slave from the

south, was not as ideal as one might have imagined.

Even though, "northern states had not adopted Jim Crow laws,

the migrants found social conditions in the north sometimes a

mirror image of what they were fleeing from in the south"

(Packard, 2003). The north was not exempt from segregation,

racism, and inequality.

In addition, some northern Negros belittled, mocked, and

rejected any affiliations with the newly emancipated southern

Negro. Some of the northern Negros appeared to express

irritation rather than admiration for the newly emancipated

southern Negro. Some northern Negros felt embarrassed by the

lack of education, the obsession with spirituals, and clothes worn

by the southern Negro. Some southern Negros retaliated by

questioning the authenticity of the northern Negro, who seems to have forgotten the price that southern slaves paid for northern Negros freedom. The division between the two groups would heighten further in some ways because the newly migrated southern Negros appeared subservient to White northerners and accepted lower wages (Packard, 2003). Even though the division between northern and southern Negros did not prevent the Harlem Renaissance's, the division did affect the relationship between the two groups. In some places, one's social, political, environmental, economic, and educational status still impacts whether a person feels accepted or rejected.

Divisions Among the Visionaries (Patrons versus Artists)

The second significant division that occurred during the Harlem Renaissance was among patrons and artists. The funding allowed for painters to network with art galleries, musicians to connect with club and record storeowners, and writers with publishers. Even though patrons were an invaluable asset to the Harlem Renaissance, controversy still arose between benefactors and beneficiaries. As much as one would like to ignore the complexities of racism, prejudice, and segregation, all of these issues were pivotal points of concern for Harlem Renaissance artists. Some Harlem Renaissance artists struggled with maintaining their racial and artistic integrity (Rhodes, 1978). Being able to maintain a copasetic relationship, between patron and artist, was challenging at times.

Some of the notable issues that developed included disparagements against artists, misappropriation of artist profits, missing ghostwriter royalties, stolen ideas, and the constant threat of funding ending if any disagreements occurred between patron and artist (Rhodes, 1978). Not every artist had a questionable relationship with patrons. Despite some of the potential negative experiences between patrons and artists, some patron and artist relationships were positive. Some patrons, like A'Lelia Walker encouraged free artistic expression and supported artist development. A'Lelia Walker was known to offer a floor in her mansion, the Dark Tower for Negro artists to plan and discuss their writings (Rhodes, 2012). Without patrons, initial and continual investments in artists, writers, actors, and musicians the Harlem Renaissance could have been a combination of individual illustrations of Negro talent, rather than a collective reflective movement.

Common Sense versus Book Smart versus Street Smart

When determining the levels of intelligence or smartness a person possess, can be quantified through tests scores and raw data or revealed through simple conversations. Living in a place like Harlem, New York, during the early 20th century, required one to be smart, for the sake of survival. However, being smart for some people requires learning, while others may be born smart. Whether a person learns to be smart or has a natural insight is irrelevant. With so many people immigrating and migrating to Harlem, New York, being cognizant of the spoken and unspoken rules of Harlem.

There are several sayings that can attributed to the discussion of what constitutes being smart, during the Harlem Renaissance era, that may be relevant today. For example, an old adage says, "Common sense ain't common." Another familiar saying reveals that, "Books can only teach you so much." Lastly, there is a saying that suggests, "In order to survive street life, you have to be street smart." These truisms may or may not be familiar to everyone, but these statements are true to someone. Living in Harlem, New York, during the Harlem Renaissance, having one, if not all of these, types of smarts could make a difference between who succeeds and who fails, who survives

and who perishes. Common sense, during the Harlem

Renaissance, was much more than choosing one's career path,

as suggested, in regards to Booker T. Washington, earlier in the

chapter. Common sense, during the Harlem Renaissance, could

possibly pertain to one's ability to make impromptu decisions that

result in the least amount of consequences or resistance. Being

book smart, during the Harlem Renaissance, could often defined

by one's ability to acquire knowledge through reading and

traditional schooling. Being book smart is often mentioned in a

complimentary way; however, being book smart could potentially

suggests that someone is lacking common sense or street

smarts. In other words, emphasis has been placed on obtaining

knowledge from books, which reveal other peoples thoughts, that

there is an inability to be smart outside of a book. Being street

smart, during the Harlem Renaissance, was suggested in regards to being a gangster. Anyone who was willing to engage in illegal activities for the purposes of money, power, and respect could only become successful, if that person had an awareness of the rules of life on the streets (aka street code). As shocking as this may be to believe, gangsterism, during the Harlem Renaissance, was strategically and adequately defined when people termed the illegal activities surrounding gangsters as "organized crime." In order to sustain a successful criminal enterprise, one has to be able to know that which is unknown to commoners and the educated. Being common sense smart, book smart, or street smart can be beneficial for any individual because each level of smartness can serve as a survival skill for anyone engaging in legal or illegal activities.

Segregation in Harlem

Segregation in Harlem was another contributing factor to the decline of the Harlem Renaissance's impact. Even though Carl Van Vetchen described Harlem as *Nigger Heaven*, Vetchen did not consider all of the people (Irish, Dutch, Jews, Germans, British, Latinos, Africans, and Americans) that made Harlem, such a paradise of excitement and enjoyment. Harlem, New York was an ideal location because the diverse population epitomized the concept of a melting pot; "a metaphor for a heterogeneous society" (U.S. Bureau of Census, 1995). In order for a society to become homogeneous, immigrants assimilating to America have to melt together to become a singular harmonious culture (U.S. Bureau of the Census, 1995). The melting pot concept focused on having people from different ethnicities live, share, and interact with one another for cultural enrichment; however, the concept failed to consider the permanent effects associated with certain cultures based on current experiences, mentalities, and history ; specifically the negative experiences.

The negative experiences of Harlemites aided in the eventual decline and demise of the Harlem Renaissance, in spite of the movement starting up north. Even though Harlem had multiple clubs for people to enjoy, most of the clubs that brought in the most money served only whites and perpetuated stereotypes of Negros. The most financially lucrative clubs operated in ways to overshadow the Harlem Renaissances' agenda to inspire a re-awakening, re-birth, or re-defining of a people, culture, and society reveals a potentially interesting truth. People seem to desire unimaginative fun and stereotypical entertainment over truth, equality, or political progress. If the most successful clubs, support segregation, then most likely the customers attending the clubs support segregation as well. The segregationist attitudes would eventually become reflective in the

216

lives of the local gangs and gangsters. For example, most gangsters, during the Harlem Renaissance, protected their respective neighborhoods, but warred and murdered other gangs and gangsters. In other words, people were not just separated in the clubs, but in their everyday lives. Even the clubs that allowed integration rarely experienced equality and diversity among the customers. How can a melting pot theory truly change those who appear to embrace segregation?

Typically, when segregation becomes normalized in certain communities, people either consciously or unconsciously choose to isolate themselves from other ethnic groups; especially in neighborhoods located in Harlem, New York, during the Harlem Renaissance. Segregation in communities often: increased violence in those communities, determined who could attend a club, resulted in constant rent increases, and impacted the ability for people to hire and pay artists to perform at parties. Eventually, the inability to gain access or participate in the nightlife of Harlem like a true Harlemite, some people began to save money and invest in blues and jazz records. In other words, a party at home could be just as enjoyable as partying in a club that you could not afford to be in anyway. Artists, like Ma Rainey and Cab Calloway could be heard on a record player, in the comfort of one's home, there was no need to pay for an artist or experience frustration about not being able to get into the Cotton Club to hear Cab Calloway perform. When a community is already separated, when times are prosperous, the likelihood of that same community coming together during hard times is improbable. Had the club scenes, gangsters, and neighborhoods been more tolerant of other ethnicities, in Harlem, New York, then maybe the impact of the Great Depression may not have been as devastating, because the same people who supported one another's success would support one another during hard times.

Imagine everyone being able to party at the same clubs, which would alleviate Negro artists anxiety about having to choose between working at an integrated club or a segregated club. More money could have been made for the artists who in turn would have spent more money on local businesses, since artists would have been permitted to eat and drink at the clubs. In addition, if gangsters, were able to share sections of Harlem and not infringe on other gangsters territories or illegal activities (like running numbers), violence would not have escalated and resulted in the deaths of people throughout Harlem. Lastly, had neighborhoods been tolerable of other ethnicities, the probability of rent constantly increasing might have been reduced in racially integrated neighborhoods. Racially integrated neighborhoods could have potentially allowed for fair practices and policies between tenants and property owners.

Older Generation versus Younger Generation

The last major contributing factor to the decline of the

Harlem Renaissance was a division between the older and

younger generations. Young and talented Negro writers of the

Harlem Renaissance intentionally chose to write about taboo

topics, not just for shock-and-awe purposes, but strategically

chosen because of the content's relevance in the daily lives of

Harlemites. The initial publication of the magazine *FIRE!!*

revealed the young groups interests. The constant

disagreements between the older and generations who created

this legendary movement eventually aided in the collapse of the

Harlem Renaissance. Not being able to agree on the direction

that a movement should go or the content that should be

discussed created division among the old school leaders like

DuBois and Washington and young school leaders like Langston

Hughes and Zora Neale Hurston. Many young writers felt

inhibited, which created a sense of frustration and rebelliousness towards the older generation leaders, who were involved in the promotion and sustainability of the Harlem Renaissance.

The Great Depression of 1929 had a devastating effect on the Harlem Renaissance, causing the movement to only last for about five years. However, other divisive factors such as: Southern versus Northern Negros, Patrons versus Artists, Common Sense versus Book Smart versus Street Smart, Segregation in Harlem, and Older Generation versus Younger Generation contributed to the demise of the Harlem Renaissance. Despite, the limited number of years that the Harlem Renaissance had to flourish; the impact of the movement has had an ever-lasting impact on American and Hip Hop culture.

Chapter 6

Rock-N-Roll Ain't Just White People's Music

Rock-n-Roll is an important part of American history and influential to Hip Hop culture's history. Rock-n-Roll's local and international popularity would begin to develop in the early 1950s. What made Rock-n-Roll appealing and relevant was the accessibility of a diverse sound of the music. Rock-n-Roll music, in the early 1950s, was a hybrid of many genres of music: spirituals, hillbilly, folk, jazz, blues, country, rhythm and blues, rock, and rockabilly music. Rock-n-Roll artists while innovatively creating new sub-genres of music. In addition, Rock-n-Roll musicians had an amazing ability to sing different styles of music, which aided in their artistic diversity; eventually garnering popularity internationally.

When some people think of Rock-n-Roll; especially those who may have a limited scope of Rock-n-Roll's diverse history, one may assume that Rock-n-Roll has and continues to be a primarily white genre of music. However, for some people the idea of Rock-n-Roll being an exclusively white genre of music may have some merit, because of the racial history of America and the delayed accessibility of Black artists in the music industry. The route to becoming a Rock-n-Roll hall of famer differed for each artist; however, race was a determining factor that impacted many artists career; especially Black artists. Because Black artists were not initially accepted by the Rock-n-Roll community, Black artists had to find innovative and creative ways to promote music and establish a fan base.

The establishment of the Chitlin' Circuit would serve multiple purposes for a Black artist; not just potential Rock-n-Roll artists. The Chitlin' Circuit was a combinational vernacular term established among Black artists that had historical and controversial significance. Chitlins' (aka chitterlings) are the small intestines of a pig. Chitlins' were often a food eaten originally by slaves and made from the left-over scraps of the pig that the slave masters did not want to eat. Slaves took the leftover scraps and turned the small pig intestines into a delicatessen. The inability for Black artists to perform on traditional circuits, like White Rock-n-Roll artists revealed why the Chitlin' Circuit was essential. For many, the Chitlin' Circuit was a strategic attempt of Black artists to make "something beautiful out of something ugly," just as slaves did during slavery (Lauterbach, 2011). Even though, Black artists were initially excluded from touring opportunities at white venues or alongside their white counterparts, the contributions of Black Rock-n-Roll artists are undeniable.

The diversity in the Rock-n-Roll era was established by pioneering record labels like Memphis and Tennessee's Sun Records, established by Sam Phillips, as well as influencers like Gerald "Jerry" Wexler, from Atlantic Records, who coined the term

"Rhythm and Blues" inspired by the melodic sounds of Ruth Brown. The evolution of record labels to include Black artists was both a triumph and a challenge for many artists. Just like artists, during the Harlem Renaissance, sought to maintain their racial integrity and artistry, so did Black Rock-n-Roll artists. Because Black musicians had limited rights in life and even more musically, conflictions would arise over sound, album covers, radio play, stage presence, performance locations (segregated venues versus integrated venues), stealing, copyright infringement, travelling and hotel accommodations, and royalties.

Checking facts and conducting one's own research, while exploring such controversial topics can be essential to understanding what is truthful and what is fictional. Despite the racial divisions of artists, during the Rock-n-Roll era, many artists who created this genre of music were more alike than different. Many artists like the Rock-n-Roll artists listed in this section, as well as many artists not listed, have dualistic similarities rooted in church and sexual innuendos. Take some time and research unknown information about each artists. Be mindful of their experiences, life-changing decisions and outcomes, and how their legacies may be perceived today. In addition to conducting research on these artists' life experiences, research the song lyrics or video (or both) listed next to the artists names as well.

- Ruth Brown (*Mama, He Treats Your Daughter Mean, 1953*)
- Big Joe Turner (*Shake, Rattle, and Roll, 1954*)
- Ray Charles (*I Got A Woman, 1954* & *Georgia On My Mind, 1960*)
- Elvis Presley (*Take My Hand, Precious Lord, 1957*)
- Jerry Lee Lewis (*Whole Lotta Shakin' Goin' On, 1957*)
- Ritchie Valens (*La Bamba, 1958*)

- Lil' Richard (*Good Golly Miss Molly, 1958*)

- Tina Turner (*Fool in Love, 1960*)

- Chuck Berry (*My Ding-a-Ling, 1972*)

Being a successful Rock-n-Roll artists was controversial, during the 1950s, because segregation and racism prevented several artists; specifically artists of color, from being accepted and acknowledged, by society at large.

Part of being accepted and acknowledged includes being given an additional name or title. For example, Elvis Presley is accepted and acknowledged as "The King of Rock-n-Roll," by Rock-n-Roll historians and his fan base. However, the title, "King," is given because of his talent and his overall success, which includes record sales locally and internationally. Historically, there seems to be an unspoken rule that the title "King of Rock-n-Roll" will never be duplicated or given to another artist, because when people accepted and acknowledged an artist with a title, that title is considered uniquely sacred. Unfortunately, not every artist, during the 1950s, was able accepted or acknowledge, during this era. Therefore, to combat any notions of irrelevance, some artists would provide their own self-affirming titles, rather than wait or rely on people to accept and affirm their relevancy in Rock-n-Roll. For example, Lil' Richard is the self-proclaimed architect of Rock-n-Roll. The title may be questionable to some people, but logical for others, because Rock-n-Roll for decades only accepted and acknowledged White artists. Therefore, the titles given to artists, like "The King of Rock-n-Roll," may have to be reconsidered; especially if *only* White people were being considered.

To be successful, during the 1950s, most minority artists; specifically Black Rock-n-Roll artists, had to be constantly mindful of how to position themselves for the best success. Often times, the best practice for establishing success included denying one's blackness. White Rock-n-Roll artists had the privilege of being white without denying one's self. In fact, White Rock-n-Roll artists could succeed in any venue and crossover without trepidation. For example, some White Rock-n-Roll artists would make a conscious effort to sound black to appeal to Black audiences, while declaring the black sound as a new trend for White audiences.

Catering to both audiences allowed record labels and artists to make double money. However, Black and Latino Rock-n-Roll artists would have to sound white, alter their appearance (sometimes), and was hardly ever allowed on their own album covers. Black and Latino Rock-n-Roll artists; specifically, struggled with deciding whether to allow white artists to re-sing their songs and change their names on the album cover to have a minimal level of success in the Rock-n-Roll music industry. With the country approaching racially charged times, decisions surrounding: disparities between races, racism, segregation, Jim Crow laws, education equality, boycotts, voting rights, lynchings, staged sit-ins, organized marches, and other social, political, and economic issues furthered the countries ability to unite and progress. The music industry would reflect these times and serve simultaneous purposes marked by progress and resistance. The term "whitewashing" is a term that was indicative of the realities of American life, during the 1950s.

The Hip Hop cultures' connection to Rock-n-Roll is the unique relationship between young people and the music, sex, and drugs. There is a continuing connection that young people have with these two styles of music; rap and rock. However, one cannot ignore the similar and repetitive trends that exist between these two genres of music. The notion and evolution of whitewashing is not confined to a singular era or genre of music; specifically music associated with African Americans; dating back since the days of slavery. Whitewashing creates insurmountable concerns about the authenticity of artistic expression, while also raising an enormity of questions about future practices and the credibility of artists. Whitewashing allowed for record labels to capitalize off a sound synonymous with the impoverished and disenfranchised without ever having to pay homage to the past and give credit to the original artists. In spite of the controversy surrounding whitewashing, that unique sound of Rock-n-Roll was still able to reach massive audiences, even if people consciously and unconsciously denied where the sound came from. Whitewashing also raises questions about whether African Americans are simply over-reaching for acknowledgement and desiring delayed credit for everything now that was never acknowledged in prior decades and centuries.

Rock-n-Roll music, nonetheless was an essential part of American history, because music was able to cross-over in ways

231

that people of different races struggled to do, in the 1950s. The combination of artists and Rock-n-Roll music produced, during this era, allowed people to listen privately to a Black or Latino sound, without having to think about the inequality that is occurring publically. Rock-n-Roll, like current Hip Hop culture has become inclusive and not exclusive. Just like Elvis is constantly and publicly considered the "King of Rock-n-Roll," Chuck Berry is simultaneously declared to be the "Father or Rock-n-Roll." Are these titles equally synonymous or an attempt to rectify an injustice and lack of credibility experienced decades before?

If one considers the current financial success and business trends of rap, one must admit that even though African Americans and minorities still serve as the majority of artists in the genre, the primary consumers and owners of rap music are not African American people. Rap sales increases even more with the occasional emergence of a White rapper. White rappers like:

Vanilla Ice, Beastie Boys (although Jewish categorized as white rappers), Mc Serch, Snow, Kid Rock, Insane Clown Posse, Paul Wall, Bubba Sparxxx, Eminem, Machine Gun Kelly, Kid Rock, Yelawolf, Mac Miller, Asher Roth, and Iggy Azalea have received great support, notable reviews, and accolades in Hip Hop locally and globally; regardless of their career longevity in the industry. Does this reality imply that Hip Hop culture (as a whole), not just the genre of rap, has become an emerging reflection of whitewashing?

Chapter 7
The Civil Rights Movement: Fantasy versus Reality

The issues that plagued America in the 1950s and 1960s

are not far removed current day issues. The horrendous and

atrocious attacks, during the Civil Rights era was not only directed

towards Black people, but also directed towards anyone who

fought for equality in America. Because the impact of the Civil

Rights Movement is extensive, significant events, dates, and

people have been listed for convenience. Take some time before

moving to the next chapter to conduct your own brief research to

identify key points of interest and connections. The reality of

America, in the 1950s and 1960s could be summarized by

referencing *13* historically distinct events:

- Protests against desegregation in schools (*Kenneth and Mamie Clark Doll Test, 1940s* & *The Brown versus Board of Education Case, 1954*)

- The Montgomery Bus Boycotts (*1955*)

- The murders of black teenagers like Emmitt Till (*1955*)

- Unlawful governmental practices led by people like FBI Director J. Edgar Hoover (*COINTELPRO, 1956*)

- Federal Marshal escorts needed (*The Little Rock 9, 1967 & Ruby Bridges, 1960*)

- The start of sit-ins (*Greensboro, NC, 1960*)

- The attack against White and Black Freedom Riders (*1961*)

- The assassination of leaders like Medgar Evers (*1963*)

- The bombing of black churches like 16th Street Baptist Church (*Church home to four little girls, 1963*)

- On-going police brutality and corruption from Police commissioners like Theophilus Eugene "Bull" Connor (*1963*)

- Race riots like the Harlem riot inspired by the killing of 16 year old James Powell by an off-duty police officer (*1964*)

- The Selma to Montgomery marches (*Bloody Sunday, 1965*)

- Assassinations of leaders: Metaphorically and physically (*Malcolm X, 1965 & Dr. Martin Luther King Jr., 1968*)

Each of these monumental events revealed why movements like the Civil Rights Movement were needed. Many of these instances could be described as terroristic in nature. Trying to understand or rationalize how people could be so hateful, racist, and bigoted would be pointless. Instead, understanding the following becomes essential:

1) Terminology (*civil versus human rights*)
2) The history of Martin Luther King Jr. & Malcolm X
3) The historical discrepancies in history (*Rosa Parks' legacy versus the legacies of Mary Louise Smith, Irene Morgan, and Claudette Colvin*)

Terminology

Often times, when discussing the Civil Rights Movement, there is an insurmountable amount of information surrounding dates, deaths, court cases, people, literature, and terminology.

With all of the information that can be researched or learned, rarely do people understand some of the words associated with such a pivotal movement or how these words are relevant to some of the issues that arise in America and surrounding countries. Terms like civil rights and human rights become essential to conversations about the complexities and issues arising, during the 1950s and 1960s. The simplistic definition for civil and human rights would be as follows:

- Civil rights are a set of rights established state-by- state, nation-by-nation, and country-by-country.
- Human rights are a set of rights given to *every* human after being born.

In other words, civil rights can change depending on where you live or travel, which is why the Civil Rights era constantly battled laws, not just in one state, but also in other states. Having to combat the atrocities committed across various states lines can be time consuming making the battle for civil rights seem eternal.

Human rights could seem overwhelming to create; however, human rights are pragmatic. Human rights are an attempt to remove the uncertainty and confliction that civil rights appear to create depending on where one lives or travels. In other words, human rights have no boundaries state-by-state, nation-by-notion, or country-by-country. Human rights are given and allowed no matter who you are, where you live, or where you travel. In other words, human rights automatically seeks to establish equality for all people at birth; eliminating the need to fight or protest for equal rights in multiple locations. Civil rights are typically focused on specific places; whereas human rights are domestic and abroad.

Dr. Martin Luther King Jr.

The fight for equality, integration, justice, and cultural progression started long before Dr. Martin Luther King Jr. became one of the essential leaders of the Civil Rights Movement. Leaders like Edgar Daniel "E.D." Nixon and the Pullman Porters, Aurelia Shines Browder (main plaintiff in the Browder vs. Gayle case, which declared segregated buses unconstitutional), and Clifford Durr (lawyer who represented C.R.M. participants) helped propel the Civil Rights Movement, before Dr. King's influence. In addition, with the help of additional organizations, like the Southern Christian Leadership Conference (SCLC) and Congress on Racial Equality (CORE), the actions and sacrifices of the Civil Rights Movement leaders and participants would not be ignored. Other notable leaders, who provided a standard for leadership for Dr. Martin Luther King Jr. included people like Dr. King Jr.'s own father, Martin Luther King Sr. Martin King Sr. took a stance against the onslaught of injustices for the sake of racial equality,

long before Dr. Martin Luther King Jr. was born. In fact, one

intriguing fact about the elder King is that his birth name was

Michael King Sr., which means that his son's birth name was

Michael King Jr. The year 1934, marked two significant life

changes for Sr.:

1) Sr. was elected to be pastor of the Ebenezer Baptist
   Church in Atlanta.
2) While celebrating a week long Baptist Alliance
   Conference in Berlin. Sr. and nine other Baptist
   ministers traveled to the Holy Land and Germany to
   further their religious knowledge (Branch, 1988).
   While on the trip, Sr. learned of the profound impact of
   the German monk Martin Luther, who wrote *The
   Ninety-Five Thesis* and led the Protestant Reformation
   (Mohn, 2012).

Sr.'s newfound knowledge inspired him to change his name (unofficially not legally) to Martin Luther King and his son's name to Martin Luther King Jr. King Jr.'s upbringing, relationship with his father (including the shared name), and understanding of Civil Rights would have a profound effect on his life, inspiring his educational goals, his political views, his religious beliefs, his non-violent approach, and his ability to show love and poise in the face of his enemies. Each of these characteristics were cultivated at various points in Dr. Martin Luther King's life, which helped create and cement his legacy.

Dr. Martin Luther King Jr. would begin to gain prominence after two monumental events. One significant event included King's leadership of the M.I.A. (Montgomery Improvement Association), affiliations with the N.A.A.C.P. (National Association for the Advancement of Colored People), and the organizational implementation of the Montgomery Bus Boycotts. King's monumental leadership was made apparent when he arrived to bail out Rosa Parks, on December 1, 1955. The second significant event that would catapult and solidify King's leadership in the Civil Rights Movement occurred, when King gave a 1957 speech at the Lincoln Memorial. The speech focused on voting rights and ballots, was given in front of a crowd estimated between 15,000 and 30,000 (Klein, 2013). The voter's rights speech would help solidify Dr. Martin Luther King Jr. as an elite leader in the fight for Civil Rights. The speech in 1957 occurred six years prior to King's famous *I Have A Dream Speech*, at the Lincoln Memorial (Klein, 2013). Dr. Martin Luther King Jr.'s participation in these two major events, in addition to organizing marches, sit-ins, and giving prolific and charismatic speeches garnered him immense support and popularity among civil rights leaders and participants.

If Dr. Martin Luther King Jr.'s legacy is depicted as a dream, then Malcolm X's legacy is a nightmare. Unfortunately, X's legacy, in comparison to King Jr.'s is disproportionate. Malcolm X's image is marred by complex inconsistencies. Even though Malcolm X's accomplishments appear to be diminished in the light of Dr. King's, Malcolm X's life was a reflection of all the people who have imperfect lives. While Dr. King was able to build and cultivate his relationships with his parents; especially his father King Sr., Malcolm X would experience a set of tragedies that would alter his reality at the age of six.

Malcolm X

The legacy of Malcolm X started at a young age, just as Dr. Martin Luther King Jr.s' did. Malcolm X was born Malcolm Little to parents Earl Little and Louise Norton Little (Haley, 1965). Malcolm's mother upbringing was controversial, because Louise's never knew her father, because a white man raped her mother (a black woman). Malcolm's mother struggled her entire life with being bi-racial and trusting white people (Perry, 1989). Malcolm's father had a religious upbringing and became a Baptist preacher. The Klu Klux Klan, constantly targeted Malcolm's father, Earl, because of his political affiliations with groups like U.N.I.A. (Universal Negro Improvement Association), outspokenness against white supremacy, and the promotion of self-efficacy (Haley, 1965).

In one instance, when Louise was pregnant with Malcolm, while living in Omaha, Nebraska, the Klu Klux Klan (KKK) vandalized the family's home (Haley, 1965). Unfortunately, Malcolm's family could not escape the KKK. While living in Lansing, Michigan, Malcolm, who was four years old at the time, family's home was burned down by the KKK (Haley, 1965). Unfortunately, Malcolm's most tragic remembrance of his father would come at the age of six. When Malcolm was six years old, his father, Earl Little, was found dead with a half-broken skull on a train track. The story surrounding Earl's death was controversial; especially considering the constant threats and attacks by Klansman. Some of the Klansman held positions of power; which included police officers, politicians, coroners, insurance men, newspaper writers.

Police reports would later raise more questions than answers for the Little family. The police report states that upon arrival to the scene Earl was still conscious and allegedly told the police, before dying, that he had accidently slipped and fallen under a streetcar (Haley, 1965). The police ruled Earl's death an accident. However, the insurance company that held Earl's life insurance policy stated that the cause of death was a suicide; exempting the company from paying benefits to the family (Perry, 1989). The local newspaper claimed that Earl died trying to jump back on a streetcar, after realizing he left his jacket on the streetcars seat (Perry, 1989). Regardless of the story of Earl Little's death, Louise (Malcolm's mother) knew that her husband's death was a homicide, not a suicide or accidental death. After, Louise, identified her husband's body at the morgue, she became depressed, negligent to the needs of her children, and eventually had a nervous breakdown. Her nervous breakdown resulted in her being declared legally insane and being committed to a mental institution (Haley, 1965).

Malcolm X's childhood and life would never remain the same. In a short period, Malcolm had lost his father and his mother; resulting in him to being sent to multiple foster homes (Perry, 1989). Malcolm, in spite of his situation, would attempt to remain focused on trying to achieve his dream of becoming a lawyer; just as his parents would have wanted. Unfortunately, Malcolm's dream was short-lived. One day while attending school, his teacher (a white woman), asked students about their dreams and goals. Malcolm shared his dream and was told by the teacher that his dream was unrealistic for a nigger and he should focus on a trade school education instead (Haley, 1965). Malcolm immediately dropped out of school and entered a life filled with mediocre jobs in various cities and would eventually led a life of crime that spanned from Boston, to Detroit, to New York. In 1946, at the age of 20, Malcolm was arrested, indicted on burglary charges and carrying an illegal firearm, and sentenced to eight to ten years (Perry, 1989).

While imprisoned, the 20-year old Malcolm's would harbor a level of resistance, resentment, and hate all the things associated with White people or whiteness. Malcolm's years in prison would be filled with self-educating himself about the history of life, the struggle of Africans to America, religious conflictions in Christian doctrine, and practices and teachings of Islam. When

26-year old Malcolm was released from prison, his life would undergo a life-changing decision. Malcolm would join the N.O.I. (Nation of Islam) and change his name from Little to X (Haley, 1965). The members of the Nation of Islam traditionally adopted the letter "X" because "X" stood for the unknown. Malcolm, like many descendants of slaves, had lost their cultural heritage because of slavery. Part of the slaves lost heritage included the loss of one's names, birth date, and cultural identity. Because slaves were forced to take on the last names of their slave owners for property claiming purposes and forced to abandon any cultural traditions that empowered or was associated with Africa, some Black people wanted to know the full truth of their history beyond what was taught, written in history books, or forced to learn (Haley, 1965). Months, after joining the Nation of Islam and being released from prison, Malcolm X would be appointed a leadership position and become a national spokesperson for the Nation of

Islam (Haley, 1965). Malcolm's appointment as the nation's newest spokesperson would be both inspiring and problematic.

As a spokesperson, Malcolm X increased the Nation of Islam's memberships; but not without controversy. About eight days after the assassination of President John F. Kennedy, Malcolm X's life and impact in the Nation of Islam would change. A news reporter asked Malcolm X about the significance of President Kennedy's death to which X replied by saying, "Kennedy's death was a case of the chickens coming home to roost." X's explanation was published nationally and viewed as being harsh and insensitive towards President Kennedy, even by fellow Nation of Islam members and leaders. Malcolm X would go on to later explain that his lackadaisical response to President Kennedy's assassination was a result of Kennedy's lackadaisical response towards the assassinations of the Four Little Girls and Medgar Evers. The childhood roots of X's hostility towards *all* whites manifested at inadequate times and moments, in Malcolm

X's life. Because of X's unapologetic lack of empathy towards the

President's death and disagreements with the Nation of Islam's

leader Elijah Muhammad, Malcolm X would be reprimanded,

demoted, and eventually banished from the Nation of Islam by

leader Elijah Muhammad in 1964 (Handler, 1964).

Although Malcolm X's demotion and separation from the

Nation of Islam was swift, tragically Malcolm X's leadership

principles and beliefs did not grow and evolve until the last year

(age 38) of his life. In the last years of X's life, he would begin to

work with civil rights leaders, rather than depreciate their efforts.

X also began to shift his perception about White people after a

reflective pilgrimage to Mecca; which occurred in 1964. While on

his pilgrimage, Malcolm X realized how much of his childhood

experiences influenced his stereotypes and demonization about

White people; just as some White people had historically done to

Blacks. X also acknowledged his ignorance, insensitivity, and his quick-tempered brashness towards *sincere* White people; most of whom were young college students who wanted to fight for human rights, not just civil rights.

Unfortunately, Malcolm X's assassination created additional controversy for his legacy. Even though, some people shared positive sentiments towards Malcolm X, others spoke frankly. *The New York Post* stated that, even Malcolm's sharpest critics recognized his brilliance—often wild, unpredictable and eccentric, but possessing promise that must now remain unrealized (Rickford, 1965). *The New York Times* (1965) said that Malcolm X was "an extraordinary and twisted man who turned many true gifts to evil purpose. His life was strangely and pitifully wasted. [He was] an unashamed demagogue whose creed was violence." Tragically, Malcolm X, like many current and future black males, would undergo controversial media depictions and vilification, before receiving a logistical view acknowledging the total portrait of his life, not just the controversial blemishes. Malcolm X struggled to create the best legacy possible, in spite of his deprived familial inheritance due to the murderous death of his father and his mother's mental instability.

While Dr. King Jr. was obtaining educational stripes (in terms of educational degrees), Malcolm had obtained his stripes as a convicted felon. These two men, ironically, would eventually exchange positions of thoughts before both of their deaths. King and many of his followers would be continually arrested for acts of civil disobedience more than twenty times, while Malcolm X would never be arrested again. Malcolm X would begin to put his faith in the world's ability to support human rights (not just the United States). King would also begin to grow increasingly resentful towards America (as a nation) for not accepting political change for equality. Evidence of King's shift in attitude and approach was prevalent on April 4, 1967, when he stood before the Riverside Church in Manhattan, New York, denouncing the Vietnam War and prophesying about God's wrath against America if America did not change its ways (Carson, 1987). King's denouncement of America's policies would become even more prevalent in 1968. About a week after Kings', April 3, 1968 *I've Been to the Mountaintop* speech to the Memphis, Tennessee sanitation workers, King was scheduled to return to Riverside Church in Manhattan, New York, on April 7, 1968 and express more disdain for his countries actions. King was planning to deliver a sermon entitled, *Why America May Go to Hell* (Smith and Meacham, 1998). Unfortunately, no one would ever hear his words, because King was assassinated on April 4, 1968. Even though both men (King and X) are often portrayed, in the media, as having an oppositional and unfriendly opinion of each other, the two men were one-in-the-same.

The media portrayals of Dr. King's and Malcolm X's relationship are questionable considering that both leaders were needed and actually complimented one another's leadership styles. Dr. King and Malcolm X had different methodically approaches to effecting change, during the Civil Rights Movement. However, both men immediately realized that they walked the same path towards equality, just in different shoes. Without each other, neither one of these men could have influenced their respective followers and created changes. Rumors suggest that King and X talked over the phone more often than people could have imagined. Also, even though their approaches were different, both men respected one another and occasional spoke over the phone about their respective positions in the fight for equality. Malcolm X felt that King's Christian rhetoric was enslaving his followers to submission, just as the slave masters had done during slavery. Malcolm X also believed that King's encouragement to be non-violent along with the promotion of sit-ins were passive attempts for any real change to occur. King believed and respected Malcolm's strength, but believed that his strength would evoke more aggression and resistance than change.

Malcolm X, in his 1964, *The Ballot or the Bullet* speech, asserts the idea that participating in sit-ins are illogical, because sitting down has no true impact on political change. Malcolm X, states explicitly that sit-ins are equivalent to castration, because anyone can sit down, and old person can sit down. Teaching people; especially young people, to sit-down creates submission; instead teach people to stand up. Malcolm X's speech evokes concerns about why a person would go to a restaurant that did not want to serve them and trust that the food or drink would not be tampered with. In other words, would you trust the waiter or cook would not spit in or place inedible objects in your food or drink? As abrasive as Malcolm X was he often complimented southern Whites in comparison to northern Whites claiming that at least in the south a Black person knows racism exists blatantly. However, up north, racism seemed hypocritical and elusive. In other words, a Black person finds difficulty discerning the intentions of White people, because some White people, up north, publicly accepted Black people, but privately despised, harassed, and secretly tormented Black people.

King would dedicate his life for civil rights; hence, the reason he would become the face of the movement. Malcolm X would dedicate his life for human rights; hence, the reason he traveled all over America and other countries teaching the same principles of universal human equality. King would solicit for unity among the races to create change substantial social, economic, and political change. However, X, believed that substantial

change started with the individual, before joining the collective.

The two opposing thoughts between these two leaders are

reminiscent of sentiments expressed by W.E.B. DuBois and

Booker T. Washington, during the Harlem Renaissance.

If King represented the American Dream, then Malcolm X

represented the American Nightmare. Despite your beliefs,

admiration, or disdain for either or both leaders, both were

needed for change to happen. For example, had X not been the

extreme alternative for progressive change by force, society may

not have chosen to accept King's request for change and

integration using peace. Just as the President needs a Vice

President, so did King and X need one another. Just as the

President and Vice President are rarely attending the same event

for fear of a two-for-one assassination, so were the interactions

between King and X. As luck would have it, only *one* picture exists of these two juggernaut leaders, King and X, together. The picture was taken on March 26, 1924 after a Senate press conference debate regarding the Civil Rights Bill. The picture was powerful, not because the two men are together in a photo, but because both men are sincerely smiling which is reflective of familiarity with one another; most likely through those unknown phone conversations between two men, who were finally able to meet. Unfortunately, as quick as the picture was taken, their exit from one another at the event was even quicker. Never let your president and vice-president go to the same location; as it makes for easy assassination attempts.

Historical Discrepancies

Possible rumors surrounding why the N.A.A.C.P might not have chosen certain people to represent the face of the Civil Rights movement range from one's physical image, character, familial roots, location, economic status, regional support. When discussing the face of any movement image; especially the Civil Rights Movement, sought to present alternative and people friendly depictions of Black people. The depictions for proper image could be viewed as controversial because some of the deciding factors did not just involve one's religious beliefs, clothing, familial relationships, education, hair texture, but also one's skin color. The terminology used to describe the preferential treatment of a person based on skin color is colorism. Even though the term is new, the concept is old. However, prior to the term colorism being used, the "Brown Paper Bag Test" was a sort of determining caste system. The decision for determining whether someone was accepted or rejected was based on whether a person's skin tone was the color of the paper bag or darker than the paper bag. If you were the same color or lighter than a brown paper bag, then you were accepted. However, if you were darker than a brown paper bag, then you were denied.

Rosa Parks' legacy an imprint on the Civil Rights Movement; specifically the Montgomery Bus Boycott, will always remain a crucial spark in the desegregation of public transportation. Stories concerning how and why Rosa Parks did not give up her seat on December 1, 1955 is a question that has caused some debate (Branch, 1988). Some stories reveal that Mrs. Parks acted alone and wanted to make a political stance, because she was tired of the injustice. Other stories suggest that Mrs. Parks did not intend to spark a movement; she was just too tired to get up and move; especially considering other seats were available. A third version of the story, explains that the bus boycott was an organized political stance. Originally, there were supposed to be three other bus boycotters who were supposed to take a stance with Rosa Parks, on December 1, 1955, but the other boycotters got scared. At the last minute, the other three bus boycotters feared going to jail, stood up, and went to the back of the bus; as advised by the bus driver, leaving Park's to either join them in the back of the bus or take a stance by herself. The third version of Rosa Park's story seems more consistent with history revealing how Rosa Parks was part of a strategic movement coordinated by the N.A.A.C.P. and Dr. Martin Luther King Jr.

Rather than dispute each version of the story, the best approach would be to start with the aftermath. What is conclusively true is that Rosa Parks was arrested; her bail was organized and paid for by Edward Daniel "E.D." Dixon and Clifford Durr, she was poised for such a nerve-wrecking situation, and photographers were ironically present to take photos of her arrest. All of these factors create a level of validity to the assertion that Rosa Parks' stance was not random; but may have been controversially organized based on other reasons; not just political change.

Have you ever heard of Irene Morgan, Mary Louise Smith, or Claudette Colvin? Maybe you have heard of some of these women, all of these women, or none of these women. Nevertheless, each of these women played a pivotal role in the admonishment of bus segregation. Morgan, Smith, and Colvin did not mimic Mrs. Parks' actions, but preceded Parks' actions. 27-year old Irene Morgan preceded Parks' stance, by about 11 years. Irene Morgan's bus boycott situation was unique because on July 16, 1944, Morgan was traveling from Virginia (a segregated bus route state) to Baltimore, Maryland (a desegregated bus route state) (Lamb, 2007).

Even though, Morgan's destination state did not segregate buses, her departure state did support segregated buses. Because Irene Morgan refused to obey the laws of Virginia and when fined by the arresting officer she ripped up the fine. She

was arrested for resisting arrest, fined, and jailed (Lamb, 2007).

Unfortunately, in spite of her attempt to evoke strategic changes,

her resistance was not enough to garner the response and

support of the N.A.A.C.P. Possible reasons, for Morgan's

exemption from becoming the face of the bus boycotts, include

her image, character, location, economic status, and the lack of

regional support. Irene Morgan was dark-skinned, most likely not

able to retain herself in a non-violent manner. In addition, Morgan

lived in a state (Maryland) that was not the same state that Dr.

Martin Luther King Jr. was appointed to lead, which made getting

political support from King or his associates difficult. In addition,

to her location not being an ideal battleground, because Morgan

was going between two destinations the difficulty in arguing

between two different state laws was not feasible. Lastly, Morgan

was poor, which added additional barriers for her to be the face of the bus boycotts. Morgan's stance and trial history would eventually be noted, but not honored or remembered as much as Rosa Parks' legacy.

Claudette Colvin was the second woman that preceded Rosa Parks' stance against segregation buses. 15-year old Colvin, was a high school student at Booker T. Washington, in Montgomery, Alabama. At a young age, Colvin, like Smith, was an active member of the youth council of N.A.A.C.P., where Rosa Parks served as an advisor (Garrow, 1985). On March 2, 1955, Claudette Colvin decided to her stance; literally 9 months and 1 day before Parks (Garrow, 1985). When asked to move and give up her seat for a White passenger, Colvin refused to give up her seat and shouted repeatedly, "It is my constitutional right to stay seated" (Garrow, 1985). After refusing to give up her seat, Colvin was arrested for disturbing the peace and fined for violating the law. Possible reasons for why the Civil Rights Movement leaders could not use Claudette as the face of the movement, because of her image, character, and economic status. Claudette was dark-skinned, yelled profusely when told to get up from her seat by the bus driver, was an un-wed and pregnant (rumored to be pregnant by an older white male), and lived in poverty. Claudette, unfortunately, for the Civil Rights Movement's agenda would have created a public relations disaster. Claudette was a 15-year-old un-wed pregnant teenager. Instead of arguing about the law, civil rights leaders would have to constantly argue against promoting sex before marriage, defending her character, and answering questions about her "baby daddy." Besides these issues, Colvin was poor and about to bring a newborn baby into an already financially strapped situation. Colvin's image was not ideal or beneficial for herself or the bus boycotts. Lastly, how could Claudette Colvin be the face of the bus boycotts? What kind of leader could she be while breast-feeding her child, struggling to achieve her education goals, and seeking inspire people (not just Black people but also White people)? To make matters worse, these assertions are not considered stereotypes, but truths, during this era, because being a teenager and pregnant was considered a sin, by most conservative Christians, who created and funded the Civil Rights Movement, while also supporting and establishing Dr. King Jr. as the leader and face of the movement?

The last woman who preceded Rosa Park's stance was a woman named Mary Louise Smith. Mary Louise Smith was a reputable young woman, who graduated from St. Jude Educational Institute, in Montgomery, Alabama. Smith was also an active participant and mentor for other young people. 18-year old Mary Louise Smith took her stance to spark a bus boycott, in the same state and year as Rosa Parks. On October 21, 1955 (about 1 month and 1 week), Smith was riding a bus in Montgomery, Alabama, when she refused to give up her seat and was arrested. Smith would have been a viable candidate to become the face of the bus boycott movement, but neither King or the N.A.A.C.P. came to her rescue. Potential reasons for Smith's inability to become the face of bus boycotts include image, economic status, and familial roots conflicted with the Civil Rights Movement's image preference. Mary Louise Smith was dark-skinned, lived in poverty, and her father was a known alcoholic (Whitaker, 2011). Smiths' economic status could potential create an issue with her dependency and dedication to the movement, because bus boycotts ultimately affected people's transportation to and from work. The bus boycotts also led to some people losing their jobs or income for not being at work on time. Another possible reasons for why Smith could not be the face of the movement includes the possibly assumption about Smith's character and assertions about her being an alcoholic like her father. Tragically, no one can pick his or her family or dictate economic status. Mary Louise Smith may not have been able to be the face of the movement; however, her legacy, like Claudette Colvin's and Irene Morgan's legacies are becoming more prominent as years pass.

Despite the degrees of separation concerning Rosa Parks, Irene Morgan, Claudette Colvin, and Mary Louise Smith each of these women provided an invaluable legacy for the fight for equality. In life, not everyone can be a (s)hero. Learning and researching about the contributions of these women and even more women who are not as known is important. No one person ever changed the world and so many people are never credited for the countless sacrifices that were made. All of these women made sacrifices in an attempt to inspire change, regardless of their situations. Being a leader or the face of any movement is difficult and requires an unfortunate image filled with fantasies of flawlessness.

The Civil Rights Movement was a strategically organized movement that included several important people whose names are known and unknown, as well as controversial historical events that are known and unknown to people. Understanding the impact of Kenneth and Mamie Clark's Doll Test results in the 1940s is important, because the study and results reveal how Black children inherited inferiority and self-hatred complexes. The complexes were developed because of segregation, racism, prejudices, and the inability to understand the spoken and unspoken pressures that Black children had to endure to obtain an education. Learning about the deaths and assaults against people, who were participating in a non-violent protests, marches, and sit-ins, is perplexing. However, nothing is more unsettling than the realization that the American Justice system, allowed for the countless and blatant murders of Black teenagers without reproach. The overwhelming devastation displayed during the

Civil Rights Movement would make any and every one fold under the pressure and wait for the next person or generation to do something. Thankfully, these tragedies inspired people to not lose hope and continue to fight for the countless people who could not fight anymore.

Even though, organizations, like the National Association for the Advancement of Colored People (N.A.A.C.P.), appeared to adopt an unspoken and controversial notion that "Image is Everything." Image became an important factor in determining who had the appeal to cross racial barriers and promote the political agenda of the movement. The marches, sit-ins, and protests were organized strategically, but so was determining the dress code for the movement. Suits, ties, Sunday dresses with buttoned sweaters, and glasses (for some), became the standard uniform for this non-violent movement. The clothing worn by those participating in the movement helped the media depict a new image for Black people, an image that was non-threatening, humane and innocent; rather than a perpetuated image of a bunch of Black rambunctious radicals. Unfortunately, this strategic stance was both essential and intrusive; especially if you were poor or did not possess a good, clean, wholesome, non-violent Christian image.

As idealistic as this notion of image being everything, the N.A.A.C.P. appeared to promote notions that if you make mistakes, lack a formal education, live in poverty, or have an imperfect family, the organization cannot include you in front-line leadership positions. The inability to use individuals like Irene Morgan, Claudette Colvin, and Mary Louise Smith could be speculations; however, the elimination and limited legacy acknowledgement of their stories is conflicting. The inability to use these women, insinuates that if you are Black (possibly dark-skinned too), flawed, poor, uneducated, and have obvious family issues, then your image will have an irreparable impact on how White people will perceive you and whether or not Black people can trust you. Unfortunately, those leading the agenda of the Civil Rights Movement forgot that nobody is perfect or has a perfect image, including Dr. Martin Luther King Jr., who had documented extra-marital affairs that were recorded by FBI's J. Edgar Hoover's COINTELPRO. This acknowledgement of extra-marital affairs is not to discredit King's legacy, but only to make a point that no one person, in any movement; especially a political movement is big enough to be exempt from human flaws or small enough to be excluded from history.

Everyone's story; especially those participating in such a monumental movement has experiences (good, bad, or indifferent) are relevant. Malcolm X, for example, came from a complex upbringing, which affected his outlook early in his childhood. Having his mother go insane over the death of his father and having his father murdered by Klansman creates enough frustration and animosity. A young Malcolm X immediately realizes the police have the power to write a fictitious account of his father's death and the local newspaper and Insurance Policy Company will easily believe the police report and even falsify the documents of the incident. All of these factors affect the chance for true justice and makes the idea of justice for all seem non-existent. In addition, the stress of knowing this truth is enough to make anyone lose hope in the justice system, White people, distrust the media, lack faith in humanity and life. As off-putting as X was in the beginning of his career, he had matured enough to realize that everyone is not hate-filled or inherently evil. There are good people; including White people, in the world who are able and willing to sacrifice time, money, and even their lives for the greater good of all humanity. The fact that leaders and followers, of all races, were willing to sacrifice their lives for equality could not be ignored.

The impact and fight for equality, in America and abroad, is just as relevant today as it were in the 1950s and 1960s. The 1950s and 1960s propelled Dr. Martin Luther King Jr. and Malcolm X; two undeniably distinct leaders with inherently different leadership strategies into the spotlight to change the world forever. Unfortunately, in life, there is an unamiable truth that one's choices are not as plentiful as one may imagine. In other words, choices become nothing more than a deduced version of "Either—Or's or Both—And's, in life. Either you like Dr. King or you like Malcolm X, but not both. The lack of choices become evident when discussing the legacies of Dr. Martin Luther King Jr. and Malcolm X.

Before continuing to read the next paragraph, please take a moment and think about how Dr. King's legacy is portrayed and honored in comparison to Malcolm X, then consider which of these leaders you preference. Most likely, based on history, holiday celebrations, and media depictions; Dr. Martin Luther King Jr. appears to be the preferred choice. Why? Hip Hop culture is a movement that reflects an inherent uninformed and indifferent view of African American history locally and globally. Most people become aware based on what someone else teaches, but true learning can only come from that which one learns for one's self. In other words, the basics principles of history are being taught, but rarely are people going beyond the basic level to learn the deeper lessons behind what is being taught. Hip Hop culture, in its inception, was created to go beyond the basic levels of awareness and seeks to evolve one's awareness to create new levels of awareness.

Artists like Public Enemy, who were known for their political and controversial content revealed the deeper lessons of life in songs like "Fight the Power" (1989) and "911 is a Joke"

(1990). Both songs revealed the false perceptions and

disproportionate realties surrounding truth and untruth. In the

song, *Fight the Power* (1989), Chuck D asserts, "Elvis was a hero

to most, but he never meant s**t to me, you see/ Straight up racist

that was simple and plain/ Motherf**k him and John Wayne/.

Then in the 1990 song, *911 is a Joke*, Chuck D reveals, "Now, I

dialed 911 a long time ago/ Don't you see how late they're

reacting/ They only come when they wanna/ So get the morgue

truck and embalm the goner/ They don't care cause they get paid

anyway." Both songs attempt to expose what is publically

promoted versus the alternative reality. For example, Elvis is

promoted as the "King of Rock-n-Roll," but how can someone be

a "King," when Elvis' only competition was White men. In

addition, 911 is promoted as a public resource for help. However,

when people, who live in low-income and crime-infested

neighborhoods, call 911 the response time of the police and ambulances appear to be slow. When the services needed are not provided, then what is the point in calling for help or even trusting that help will be there when you need it? Public Enemy's song was created in 1990, but still has relevancy. On June 19, 2008, a 49-year-old woman named Esmin Green, entered a New York City psychiatric emergency room hospital in need of help (*CNN*, 2008). After not being seen by doctor, nurse, or attendees for nearly 24 hours, the woman collapsed and died on the waiting room floor from blood clots that passed from her legs and traveled through her blood stream to her lungs (*CNN*, 2008). No one (including the doctors, nurses, attendees, or security guards) noticed her lying on the floor dead for more than an hour. Documenting the inconsistencies and inequalities in society is what the Civil Rights Movement did and what the Hip Hop generation aspires to do.

Besides speaking against injustice, the Hip Hop culture reveals honest levels of support and respect for the legacies of Dr. Martin Luther King Jr. and Malcolm X. Both leaders, King Jr. and X, are respected within Hip Hop culture; however, Hip Hop has a stronger affinity towards Malcolm X. In a 1991 song called *Words of Wisdom*, Tupac (2Pac), rhymed:

No Malcolm X in my history text, why is that?/ 'Cause he tried to educate and liberate all blacks./ Why is Martin Luther King in my book each week? / He told blacks, if they get smacked, turn the other cheek./

Malcolm X's life is revered in Hip Hop culture because he was an out-cast from the start. The fact that X: was being raised by a single parent mother (briefly) because his father was murdered, orphaned because of his mother's mental health, a convicted criminal, was a misunderstood leader, and was not the preferred choice of a Christian society, but embraced by the streets makes

X relatable to those who created and sustain Hip Hop culture. The Hip Hop generation includes many people who can identify with the same historical experiences of Malcolm X. Malcolm X, for many, Hip Hop enthusiasts, has become the personification of what life is for potential leaders who grew up with no hope and all odds against them. Malcolm X represents what a reformed thug/thugette could be if he or she chooses to go legit and impact the world positively without ever forgetting their past, which is similar to the experiences of many rap artists.

Many rappers have also mimicked Malcolm X's famous 1964 photo, which shows X "looking out of the window, in a suit, while holding a rifle." The famous photo and pose has been used by many rap artists for album cover artwork and customized T-shirts. Other artists have re-created the same pose for photo shoots or referenced the pose in a rap verse (as Nicki Minaj did in 2014, in the controversial single *Lookin' A** Nigga*). Not only has

Hip Hop culture adopted the pose of Malcolm X, X's quote, "By

Any Means Necessary," is often indoctrinated in the minds of

many Hip Hop fans without a conclusive understanding. In other

words, most people do not know the totality or intentions of

Malcolm X's most quoted phrase, which often served as a tactical

approach to injustice. Malcolm X believed that people should do

whatever they have to-"by any means necessary," to maintain

equality and justice; especially when a person's full rights as a

human being are being violated. Malcolm X's quote was never

designed to be used to justify random acts of violence against

people based on retaliation or hate. Unfortunately, extremists

with negative intentions and justifications often quote X's familiar

phrase incorrectly.

Elements of the Civil Rights Movement unspoken motto,

"Image is everything," is also visible within current Hip Hop

culture. Most rappers have an insatiable obsession with

materialism and an over-sized ego that believes in showing money, not saving money. Since the official announcement of a Hip Hop movement, in New York, in the mid-1970s, image has been an important part of the trend setting styles of the movement. Image, in Hip Hop culture, has dictated what clothing brands are acceptable and unacceptable. For example, if a person asked for a pair of Timberland boots, then that person wants a pair of Timberland boots, not John Deere boots. Hip Hop culture, like most of society struggles to find a common ground of support for both legacies.

Even though, some rap fans may share Tupac's (2Pac's) sentiments about King's passiveness in comparison to X's aggression, both approaches provided a sense of hope for both sets of followers. The conflictions of King's and X's legacy are reflective when considering the following statement: There is nothing weak about being non-violent and turning the other cheek and true strength is not defined by a gun or physicality. Since the devastating assassinations, murders, and deaths of Dr. Martin Luther King Jr.(died 1968), Malcolm X (died 1965), and countless other known and unknown leaders and participants and fighters for equality and change, many people still wonder if human and civil rights will ever be accomplished in their lifetimes. The same concerns that plagued Civil Rights leaders, in the 1950s and 1960s, plagued a new generation of leaders who would ultimately inspire movements like The Black Arts Movement and The Black Panther Party of Self-Defense.

Chapter 8

The Rise of Post-Civil Rights Movements: The Emergence of The
Black Arts Movement & The Black Panther Party

With the rise of violence, murders, and assassinations
against Civil Rights leaders, protestors, and organizers, artists
(specifically musicians, poets, and playwrights) attempted to use
their prowess purposefully to evoke change. Artists like Nina
Simone provided a profound song to address the issues, in 1964,
called *Mississippi Goddam!!* The song lyrics shouts:

> Alabama's gotten me so upset/ Tennessee made lose my
> rest/ And everybody knows about Mississippi Goddam/
> Can't you see it/ Can't you feel it/ It's all in the air/ I can't
> stand the pressure much longer/ Somebody say a
> prayer/...Hound dogs on my trail/ School children sitting in
> jail/ Black cat cross my path/ I think every day's gonna be
> my last/ Lord have mercy on this land of mine/ We all
> gonna get it in due time/ I don't belong here/ I don't belong
> there/ I even stopped believing in prayer.

As disturbing and damning as Simone's words are, Simone's lyrics are blatantly honest and reflective of many people's thoughts and concerns, in 1964. Part of being a great artist is maintaining relevance and being a voice for the people and a voice that speaks against injustice; even if speaking honestly costs one's career to end. Simone's words became the precedence and inspiration for other artists that sought to be more than just a voice of entertainment, but an impactful voice of enlightenment.

The Black Arts Movement (aka B.A.M.) was a movement that emerged at a pivotal moment, during the Civil Rights Movement. Amiri Baraka (born Everett LeRoi Jones) founded the Black Arts Repertory Theatre in Harlem, New York, and started The Black Arts Movement; which was the same year of Malcolm X's assassination (Salaam, 1997). The Black Arts Movement is often dubbed the "Second Harlem Renaissance," because the primary goals was to reinvigorate Black people with literature. The Black Arts Movement was a hybrid movement that focused on fusing poetry with politics. Amiri Baraka wanted to use the beauty of poetry to expose the ugliness in politics, during the 1960s and 1970s. B.A.M.'s premier poem, *Black Art*, written by Amiri Baraka, would not only define the issues of the movement, but also ignite a barrage of controversy. A summarized snippet of the poem reads as follows:

> Poems are bulls**t unless they are
> teeth or trees or lemons piled
> on a step. Or black ladies dying
> of men leaving nickel hearts
> beating them down.../
> F**k poems...Stinking Whores!
> We want poems that kill.
> Assassin poems, Poems that shoot guns.
> Poems that wrestle cops into alleys
> and take their weapons leaving them dead.

The particular poem, *Black Art*, was strategically written by Amiri Baraka written to evoke a response from listeners. Amiri Baraka uses purposeful profanity to ignite a sense awareness for the reader. The Black Arts Movement was designed to paint an authentic picture of the social, economic, and political issues that were plaguing Black people. B.A.M. was transparent in these truths and not sought not to romanticize the realities of the on-going struggle for freedom and equality.

The Black Arts Movement included other notable leaders, thinkers, writers, and poets, like Nikki Giovanni, Larry Neal, Addison Gayle, Hoyt Fuller, Maya Angelou, and Sonia Sanchez. These artists also used their voices to provide a level of consciousness for people; specifically Black people who had become immobilized with fear, due to the assassination of Malcolm X and the blatant abuse against the marchers in Selma on Bloody Sunday. Even though the movement ended in 1975 and could be described as short-lived, the Black Arts Movement

revived the essence of the Harlem Renaissance's poetry. The

Black Arts Movement created a new form of poetry that requires

reaction and encourages a generation of conscious rappers to not

just talk on the microphone, but speak truth to power.

The Black Panther Party

In 1966, in Oakland, CA, two revolutionary Black

Nationalist named Huey P. Newton and Bobby Seale founded

The Black Panther Party for Self-Defense (later shortened to The

Black Panther Party) (Wan Deburg, 1992). The Black Panther

Party was one of the most controversial youth inspired

movements, in American history. The primary agenda was to

establish economic, social, and political quality across gender and

color lines. The group would be inspired to wear all black, for a

sense of unity and empowerment, as well as implore militaristic approaches of resistance. Similar methods and strategies were borrowed from Malcolm X; especially the phrase, "By Any Means Necessary." When threatened with injustice, The Black Panther Party would stand and fight, rather than walk away. To solidify the group's agenda a "Ten-Point Program" was implemented. The ten rules included the following decrees (Van Deburg, 1992):

1) We want freedom. We want power to determine the destiny of our Black community.
2) We want full employment for our people.
3) We want an end to the robbery by the capitals of our Black community.
4) We want decent housing fit for the shelter of human beings.
5) We want education for our people that exposes the true nature of this decadent American society. We want education that teaches us our true history and our role in present-day society.
6) We want all Black men to be exempt from military service.

7) We want an immediate end to police brutality and murder of Black people.

8) We want freedom for all Black men held in federal, state, county, and city prisons and jails.

9) We want all Black people, when brought to trial to be tried in court by a jury of their peer group or people from their Black communities; as defined by the Constitution of the United States.

10) We want land, bread, housing, education, clothing, justice, and peace.

The "Ten-Point Program" would lead and inspire the actions of The Black Panther Party. These of the initial goals of The Black Panther Party was to empower Black People, combat injustice without compromise, promote self-determination, and protect the community against danger.

Most of the danger plaguing the community in the late 1960s involved the assassination and murder of Black leaders, governmental conspiracies, unlawful police arrests, and police brutality incidences, which often resulted in the murder of a Black person. Police brutality and murder were already heightened issues among Black people, but the issue increased even more after the 1968 assassination of Dr. Martin Luther King Jr., which caused several riots throughout America. These riots would later be dubbed "The Holy Week Uprising" and occurred in multiple cities like: Washington, D.C., Baltimore, Maryland, Louisville, Kentucky, Kansas City, Missouri, Chicago, Illinois, and Wilmington, Delaware (Levy, 2011).

Even after Dr. King Jr.'s assassination and "The Holy Week Riots," additional deaths would occur within The Black Panther Party. The controversial deaths of an Oakland Black Panther member Bobby Hutton (died 1968) and a Chicago Black Panther leader Fred Hampton (died 1969) sparked outrage with the organization. The deaths were considered controversial because both men were killed, while allegedly un-armed, during police raids (Ward and Wall, 1988). Hutton and Hampton's deaths along with countless other Black Panther Party members caused the Black Panther Party to become more aggressive in their stance to combat police brutality.

The increase of assassinations of Black leaders, like Malcolm X, Dr. King Jr., and Hampton, as well as the deaths of young people like Hutton, The Black Panthers distrust and resistance against local police, state troopers, and governmental agencies was heightened. Despite the controversial deaths of past and recent leaders and members of The B.P.P., The Black Panther Party and the leaders grew stronger in leadership and membership. The Black Panther Party became fearless against resisting inequality and supporters of retaliating against local, state, and governmental officials. The Black Panther Party would continue to gain influence in communities across the nation and memberships. Within four years, The Black Panther Party had increased substantially and spread from Oakland, California to 68 other cities (Van Debug, 1992). With each controversial death and the onslaught of failed political strategies, approaches to change, The Black Panther Party members, throughout the various cities, became a self-determined organization that became a prominent threat against America. The threat of the Black Panther Party's influence made the group a target and public enemy number one; especially in the eyes of FBI's J. Edgar Hoover.

Pivotal programs were developed to increase self-determination for Black Panther Members and the communities. The Black Panther Party created health organizations to provide families with healthcare. Another important program that the BPP developed, in 1969, was a Free Breakfast Program, so that school age children would be guaranteed free breakfast before school every day (Van Debug, 1992). The initial contributions and organizational programs of The Black Panther Party was

innovative and timely. Providing people in the community with

basic needs cannot only empower the members of the

organization, but the community at large. With more apparent

communal presence and increases in membership, The Black

Panther Party would begin to endure more scrutiny and

governmental observation; specifically from FBI's J. Edgar

Hoover. Hoover's COINTELPRO conducted surveillance of the

group's activities and meetings, falsified documents, as well as

infiltrated the organization using informants, which created

dissension and distrust among The Black Panther Party leaders.

After conducting surveillance and gathering information on the

groups' daily activities, FBI's J. Edgar Hoover would eventually

label The Black Panther Party as one of the greatest threats

against America's internal security (Churchill and Wall, 2002).

Around the mid-1970s, amid: the constant harassment of local police and FBI surveillance, rumors of illegal activities involving extortion, drug dealing, questionable affiliations with gangs, and internal organizational strife at various Black Panther branches, membership began to decline (Ward and Wall, 2002). However, the most damning issue surrounding the Black Panther Party would be the suspected drug dealing and alleged extortion practices of the organization (Ward and Wall, 2002). Some researchers reveal that The Black Panther Party did sell drugs and extort merchants, as well as drug dealers, for personal gain. However, contradictory research reveals The Black Panther Party did not engage in drug dealing or extortion practices. The organization did; however, charge drug dealers a rent to sell drugs on the corners of the neighborhood, as well as offer security protection for local merchants for a fee. Allegedly, The Black Panther Party was more concerned with the fulfillment of the "Ten Point" goals rather than concerns about the methods applied; hence the notion, *By Any Means Necessary*. The money earned from charging drug dealers rent and merchants could be used to fund potential projects and programs. Because The Black Panther Party was being constantly scrutinized publically, privately, politically, and by FBI director J. Edgar Hoover, many members of the group and staunch supporters abandoned the movement.

The history of The Black Panther Party is conflicting. Some people compliment the youth inspired organization for resisting and combating a systemic structure of racism that appeared to move slow to the needs of Black people. Others complained that The Black Panther Party was nothing more a fascist group that: supported violence, endorsed cop-killing, and promoted hate-filled beliefs and rhetoric about White people and governmental authority; resulting in the group being called the

"Black KKK," by many critics. Unfortunately, trouble with the law, arrests, assassinations, alleged murder cover-ups, and the controversial death of Huey P. Newton (who had become a drug addict towards the end of his life), would eventually cause The Black Panther Party's influence to disintegrate and the organizations' legacy to be eradicated from not just Black history, but American history.

The legacy of The Black Arts Movement and the Black Panther Party would be resurrected by a Hip Hop's Forefather, a man named Gil Scott-Heron. Heron would evolve the patented phrase "By Any Means Necessary" and create a new speech prose infused slogan, in 1971, entitled *The Revolution Will Not Be Televised*. A snippet of Gil Scott-Heron's work states:

You will not be able to stay home, brother./ You will not be able to plug in, turn on and cop out./ Because the revolution will not be televised./

296

The revolution will not give your mouth sex appeal./ The revolution will not make you look five pounds thinner, the revolution will not be televised, Brother./ There will be no pictures of pigs shooting down brothers.../There will be no pictures of Whitney Young.../ Green Acres, The Beverly Hillbillies, and Hooterville Junction will no longer be so god damned relevant,/ and women will not care if Dick finally screwed Jane./ The revolution will not be televised./

There will be no highlights on the eleven o'clock news/ and no pictures of hairy armed women liberationists/ and Jackie Onassis blowing her nose./ The revolution will not be right back after a message about a white tornado, white lightning, or white people./ You will not have to worry about a dove in your bedroom, a tiger in your tank, or the giant in your toilet bowl./

The revolution will not go better with Coke./ The revolution will not fight the germs that may cause bad breath./ The revolution will put you in the driver's seat./ The revolution will not be televised,/ will not be televised, will not be televised,/

will not be televised./ The revolution will be no re-run brothers/ The revolution will be live.

Heron's words would become the foundational bridge that introduces Hip Hop culture to the world. Hip Hop culture's founding generation are the direct sons and daughters of the Civil Rights generation. Therefore, movements like the Black Arts Movement and The Black Panther Party become blueprints for the Hip Hop generations' voice.

Chapter 9

Soulless to Soulful: The Impact of Berry Gordy & Motown on Hip Hop Culture

Only one word could be used to define the soul era and soul music; timeless, and there is only one person who could be considered the architect of soul music; Berry Gordy Jr. Being an innovative architect of any musical genre can be difficult; however, Berry Gordy attempted to achieve musical ingenuity at a time when racial tensions were heightened. "Gordy helped to heal the country's fractured psyche by capturing the white American ear with melodies of love and brotherly cooperation that were sweetly subversive" (Dyson, 2014). Gordy's vision and decision to create a legitimate record company, during such a tension-filled period, could either be the best or worst decision of his life. In other words, Berry Gordy Jr. would have to ask himself some pertinent questions, before and throughout his career, to determine the impact and relevancy of his work. Some of the questions, Gordy Jr., probably asked himself:

1) How can I help create a music powerful enough to make people feel better, when things seem the worst?
2) Should music have a political voice to address the issues that currently exist?
3) How can I ensure longevity in this business and for the artists I sign to my label?

Berry Gordy Jr. would answer these questions, while also considering additional concerns and issues. Gordy's vision and strategies implemented would become a template for future record label executives and owners. Learning how to crossover cultural boundaries to achieve success in the music industry takes practice and insight. Gordy Jr.'s template for success would become legendary and monumental; especially for Black record label owners.

Berry Gordy Jr.'s rise as an innovative record label owner started with humble, but controversial beginnings. Gordy Jr.'s great grandfather was a white plantation owner and his great grandmother a slave, from Atlanta Georgia (Aronson, 2001). Gordy's familial complexities surrounding race would most likely influence how Gordy Jr. saw the world; especially through music. Gordy Jr. was born and raised in Detroit, Michigan and quickly learned from his father the importance of discipline and hard work (Early, 2004). However, education would take a backseat to pursuing one of his dreams; boxing. For Gordy Jr. boxing fulfilled two purposes: becoming his dream job and making him money. Gordy Jr. dropped out of high school, in the eleventh grade to become a professional boxer and make money (Early, 2004). Gordy Jr.'s boxing career was short-lived, after just 15 fights. Even though Gordy Jr. was undefeated, he realized that the money he was making was not worth the potential injuries that could be inflicted (Early, 2004).   Before Gordy Jr. could begin too

pursue his second dream, which was music; specifically writing

music, he was drafted into the army (Early, 2004).

Once Berry Gordy Jr. returned home from the war, he got

married, and used the money from the army and a loan from his

father and bought a record store called 3-D Record Mart. Owning

the record store enhanced Gordy Jr.'s interest and obsession with

music; specifically writing music. Unfortunately, Gordy Jr.'s

record store was not providing enough money for Gordy Jr. and

his family and closed after two years. Gordy Jr. would eventually

find employment and began working for Wayne Ford Assembly

Plant, while simultaneously keeping his musical passions alive by

writing for and promoting local artists (Aronson, 2001). While

working at the factory, Gordy Jr. would begin to expand his vision

for music. Now, Gordy Jr. would wanted to open a record label where he could build a musical empire, just like other White and Jewish record label owners.

However, Gordy Jr. realized that owning his own music label would not be easy, because the music business for many aspiring Black artists, writers, producers, promoters, and potential record label owners was just as racially divided as society. Therefore, his record label must be more than just a place where artists make music, but a place where artists could be accepted. Gordy Jr. would create a music label that made artists; especially Black artists, feel like family rather than just a money-making machine. The company would become a family affair and implore similar business practices that Gordy Jr. learned while working at the Wayne Ford Assembly Plant.

On January 12, 1959, after saving some of his money and borrowing about 800.00 dollars from friends and family, Gordy Jr. opened his first record label company called, Tamla Records.

The name Tamla was inspired by the Debbie Reynolds film called *Tammy* (Early, 2004). Gordy Jr. experienced moderate success running the record label from family and friends apartments; however, the success was not definitive like he envisioned. Therefore, on April 14, 1960, Gordy Jr. created a second label called Motown Records, that would blend the roots of Detroit's nickname "Motor" and "Town." The new record label name, Motown Records, would create a well-needed change to the trajectory of Berry Gordy Jr.'s musical ingenuity and success, which cemented his legacy in the music business.

Even though Berry Gordy's *initial* ventures were not as successful as his White and Jewish record label counterparts, Motown's success would improve quickly. Because of record sales *and* Gordy Jr's ability to identify and resonate with the experiences of Black people; specifically Motown's artists, the labels success was undeniable and unmatched. Motown Records possessed, in comparison to other record labels or moguls, an understanding and sense of Black culture and the Black experience, during a racially divided time. Motown's ability to connect with the artist as a person and not just as a means of monetary gain, made the label seem ideal. Understanding Black people; especially artists in the 1950s and 1960s, was essential for any record labels success. Many Black artists struggled, when signed to White or Jewish record labels, because the owners appeared to care more about making money. In addition, more promotion and support was given to White label mates. Lastly, Black artists struggled with trying to get White or Jewish label record owners to understand, care, and realize how stressful performing in segregated venues were for Black artists. Making money is great, but having your life threatened before, during, and after a performance was nerve-wrecking. In addition, Black artists had to deal with being segregated in country and isolated constantly from radio play, which often affected many Black artists' esteems, careers, and music. In addition to the psychological stressors experienced by Black artists, during the Civil Rights era, many artists were not being fairly compensated for their record sales. Black artists always were fighting for royalties, payments, and song choices, styles, and negotiating touring schedules and locations. Unfortunately, black artists believed that most record labels were nothing more than a business; a business that was all about money and not about the person singing the music.

Black artists wanted a label to call home; a label that understood the artists and the artists' needs. Gordy Jr.'s label became more than a business; the label was a home and made artists feel like family. Having a label that used a family structure style approach to business allowed Gordy Jr. to spend more time focusing on music and artist development, rather than recruitment. Recruitment was easy for Gordy Jr.'s label, because artists would recruit other artists. Motown artists would share their experiences working with Gordy, explain how Gordy Jr. differed from other record label owners, and how family-oriented the label seemed. The shared experiences would often motivate other Black artists to sign a deal to record with Motown.

The Motown record label would serve as a home that focused on caring for the artists as people and developing artists so they could have longevity in the music industry and not just be one-hit wonders. Motown Records, under the direction of Berry Gordy Jr., provided a foundation for not just great chart-topping music, but also for new formed perceptions about Black people; especially young Black people. Gordy Jr. realized that creating a successful music business required a similar business approach, just like the one used by the Wayne Ford Assembly Plant. Gordy Jr. realized that if he were to implement the same business principles; using an assembly line approach to developing and promoting music artists. Gordy Jr. would develop each artist in a timely fashion, so that when one artist succeeded the next artist would follow that success and so on and so on. Gordy Jr. would not rush to release an artist's record, because he wanted his artists to have longevity in their career. Gordy Jr. believed that his process of cultivating an artist would benefit not just him, but the artist.

Berry Gordy Jr. was known to have high expectations and restrictions for his artists. Artists were developed not just musically, but professionally and personally. Artists were taught to behave as if someone is always watching; therefore, artists were taught how to behave, speak, eat, and dress (Aronson, 2001). Other restrictions included no drugs, smoking, late night rendezvous that could jeopardize an artist's showmanship. Berry Gordy Jr. signed various musical acts, one of which included one of his closest friends, William "Smokey" Robinson. Robinson was also a musical genius that had an amazing ability to write, record, and perform music. The two friends, Berry and Smokey would help elevate the label to stratospheric levels of success creating a new surname for the label called "Hittsville, USA." The Motown Record label would record countless number one and top ten records. Motown's success was not just attributed to support by black audiences, but white audiences as well. With every number one record produced, talented artists begin to encroach the label headquarters by the droves.

Berry Gordy Jr. provided a seemingly soulless America that was under extreme scrutiny for racial inequality and the assassination of Black leaders, with a redemptive soul filled sound that would modernize the sound of spirituals into soul music. Soul music would connect the most complex feelings of a society collectively and independently by exploring elements of pain, happiness, sorrow, uncertainty, desire, faith, love, struggle, relationships, and despair. Berry Gordy's label included iconic artists like Stevie Wonder, The Marvelettes, The Temptations, The Jackson 5, The Supremes, Mable John, Eddie Holland, Jackie Wilson, Marvin Gaye, The Miracles, the Four Tops, Martha Reeves, Glady's Knight and the Pips, Tammi Terrell, Mary Wells, and the Vandellas.

Take some time and research some of the most prominent, most of who were Motown artists, who emerged, during the Civil Rights Movement. Be mindful of their experiences, life-changing decisions and outcomes, and how their legacies may be perceived today. In addition to conducting research on these artists' life experiences, research the song lyrics or video (or both) listed next to the artists names as well.

- Jackie Wilson (*Shout, 1959*)

- Sam Cooke (*A Change is Gonna Come, 1964*)

- Aretha Franklin (*RESPECT, 1967*)

- James Brown (*I'm Black and I'm Proud, 1968*)

- Primettes/Diana Ross and The Supremes (*Love Child, 1968*)

- The Temptations (*Cloud Nine, 1968*)

- The Jackson 5 (*ABC, 1970*)/ Michael Jackson *Dirty Diana, 1988*)

- Otis Redding (*Ain't No Sunshine, 1971*)

- Marvin Gaye (*What's Going On, 1971*)

- Stevie Wonder (*Higher Ground, 1973 & Superstition, 1973*)

Being a successful record label that has longevity is not easy; especially for a Black record label, during the Civil Rights era. Artists who were not signed to Motown Records would endure scrutiny, struggle, and hardships, while attempting to pursue their dreams in the music industry. Many artists signed to Motown, initially, embraced Berry Gordy Jr.'s family structured business model; however, controversy would begin to rise between Gordy Jr. and other artists.

There is an old saying, "Competition breeds contempt." These words epitomized that which made Motown Records successful and what caused the eventual decline of the label, under the direction of Berry Gordy. As reviewed, in the brief research conducted, one is able to notice some of the controversy and competition surrounding the artists mentioned on the bulleted list. Sustaining a successful record label can be difficult; especially if the record label owner is a pioneer and seeks to not just make music, but change music and the music industry. In addition to the stress that comes with running a business, rumors of affairs, preferential treatment, being compared to white artists, drug addictions, turmoil within musical groups, disagreements about lyrical content, un-fulfilled contractual obligations, financial disputes, conflicts of interest developing constantly, and

dishonesty would eventually effect the legendary record label.

One June 8, 1988, Berry Gordy Jr. decided to sell his initial

800.00-dollar investment, the legendary Motown Record

Corporation, to MCA Records for 61 million dollars (Aronson,

2001).

Despite the racial divisions of artists, during the Civil

Rights era, many soul artists made a point to use their music as a

tool to influence people's lives. Each artist's personal

experiences (good, bad, and indifferent) provided audiences then

and now with an opportunity to realize that no one person goes

through struggles alone. Being able to hear songs, during this era

that expressed a range of emotions, made soul music special.

The fact an artist could chose to have their music inspire listeners

on all levels; even levels of controversy surrounding politics and race, which could be costly to an artists' career, was liberating for the artist and the listener.

The choice to make one's music political in any way could create backlash and destroy an artists' career. This is why many artist; especially Black artists chose not to publically reveal their thoughts, even though privately Black artists may have felt a sense of rage for all of the injustices that were occurring throughout the United States, in the 1950s and 1960s. This truth is not only evident historically, but also presently, and does not discriminate against an artist ethnicity.

Do you remember the Dixie Chicks? In case you are unfamiliar with the group, the Dixie Chicks were an American country band that expressed disdain for George W. Bush's stance on war and the invasion of Iraq on March 10, 2003. "During a London concert, 9 days before the March 19, 2003 invasion of Iraq, lead vocalist Maines (of the Dixie Chicks) told the audience:

""We don't want this war, this violence, and we're ashamed that the President of the United States (George W. Bush) is from Texas" (Thompson, 2014). The Dixie Chicks stance against the war caused a public outrage, in the United States. A huge percentage of Americans and media outlets boycotted and publically denounced the band for their opinions. Taking a stance against injustice may cost an artist many things; especially a Black artist, during the Civil Rights era. A Black artist was already dealing with setbacks, within and outside the music industry; therefore, adding politics would surely cause further decline of an artists' career.

Hip Hop artists, like those of previous genres are susceptible to the same personal experiences, career triumphs, and career failures of their predecessors; in spite of controversial lyrics being beneficial for some rap artists. Hip Hop culture, like the previous genres of music, have experienced rejection before acceptance. The legacy and impact of Berry Gordy's rise to power, inspired many Hip Hop moguls and record labels. For example: Russell Simmons and Rick Rubin's Def Jam Record Label in the early 1980s, J (James) Prince's Rap-A-Lot Records in the late 1980s, Sean "Puffy Daddy" Comb's Bad Boy Record Label in the 1990s, and other notable young African American record label owners across the United States would use Gordy Jr.'s blueprint for success to establish their own success in Hip Hop culture. Simmons, Rubin, Prince, Combs, and others signed some of the best and greatest Hip Hop artists and produced records for artists using an assembly line approach. The essence of East coast Hip Hop was derived in the sounds of Def Jam, Rap-A-Lot, and Bad Boy artists; as well as the emerging sounds of West coast, Southern, and Mid-West Hip Hop.

Not only is Berry Gordy Jr.'s fingerprint on the success of most successful Hip Hop record labels, so are the artists of the soul era. Stevie Wonder's ability to paint vivid pictures of life, in spite of his blindness, is evident in several rap artists lyrics. Artists like Curtis Mayfield and The Temptations provide insight about pimping and drug culture, in their music. However, no soul artists was more influential than the Godfather of Soul, James Brown. James Brown is the most sampled artist in Hip Hop culture; not just acoustically, but fashionably as well. James Brown was able to maintain an addictive and funky sound in his music, create relevant lyrical content, and exhibit a level of confidence (aka swagger) that rivaled men and women alike. James Brown not only made being Black and proud acceptable, but to not be ashamed to wear your wealth (clothing, jewelry, and shoes). James Brown, The Godfather of Soul, was the prototype for what success could look like when a person who has nothing comes into something.

List of References

Abrahams, Roger D. (1985). *African American Folktales: Stories of Black Traditions in the New World*. New York: Pantheon.

Afryea, Alexandra. (2014). *TV One (US TV network)* series Celebrity Crime Files: Lady Gangster.

Aronson, Virginia. (2001). *The History of Motown*. Philadelphia: Chelsea House.

Bisson, Terry. (2005). *Nat Turner: Slave Revolt Leader*. Philadelphia: Chelsea House Publishers.

Black, Samuel. (2006). *The Harlem Renaissance Poets and Musicians*. TimBookTu.

Retrieved from http://www.timbooktu.com/spence/harlem.htm.

Blanc, Serge (1997). *African Percussion: The Djembe*. Paris: Percundanse Association.

Bradford, Sarah Hopkins (orig. pub. 1886), (1961). *Harriet Tubman: The Moses of Her People*. New York: Corinth Books.

Bradford, Sarah Hopkins (orig. pub. 1869), (1971). *Scenes in the Life of Harriet Tubman*. Freeport: Books for Libraries Press.

Branch, Taylor. (1988). *Parting the Waters: America in the King Years 1954-64*. New York, New York: Simon & Schuster Paperbacks.

Bryant, Jonathan M. (2002). Klu Klux Klan in the Reconstruction. History & Archaeology: Civil War & Reconstruction, 1861-1877. New Georgia Encyclopedia. Retrieved from http://www.georgiaencyclopedia.org/articles/history-archaeology/ku-klux-klan-reconstruction-era.

Bundles, A'Lelia. (2003). *On Her Own Ground: The Life and Times of Madam C.J. Walker*. New York: Scribner.

Chepesiuk, Ron. (2012). *Queenpins: Notorious Women Gangsters from the Modern Era*. Strategic Media Books Publishing. Retrieved excerpts from http://www.crimemagazine.com/best-madam-america.

Clayborne Carson, David J. Garrow, Gerald Gill, Vincent Harding, and Darlene Clark
Hine, eds. (1987). *The Eyes on the Prize Civil Rights Reader*. New York:
Penguin Books.

Chang, Larry and Terry, Roderick (2007). *Wisdom for The Soul of Black Folk*.
Washington, D.C: Gnosophia Publishers.

Churchill and Vander Wall (2002). *The COINTELPRO Papers: Documents from the FBI's
Secret Wars Against Dissent in the United States*. South End Press.

CNN. (2008). *Tape shows woman dying on waiting room floor*. Retrieved from
http://www.cnn.com/2008/US/07/01/waiting.room.death/indexhtml?eref=rs.

Cockrell, Dale (1997), *Demons of Disorder: Early Blackface Minstrels and their World*.
Cambridge University Press: Cambridge Studies in American Theatre and
Drama.

Conrad, Earl (1942). *Harriet Tubman: Negro Soldier and Abolitionist*. New York:
International Publishers.

Cullen, Frank, et al. (2007). *Vaudeville, Old & New: An Encyclopedia of Variety
Performers in America, Vol. 1*. New York: Routledge.

Davis, Arthur P. (1974). *From the Dark Tower: Afro-American Writers, 1900-1960*,
Howard University Press.

Davis, Thomas. Modern Voices. Africans in America | Part 1 | Resource Bank Contents –
PBS.

Douglass, Frederick. (1848). The Hutchinson Family—Hunkerism. *North Star, Volume 1,
no.44*.

Du Bois, W. E. B. (1903). The Souls of Black Folk. New York: Dover Publications.

Du Bois, W.E.B. (1891). Enforcement of the Slave Trade Laws
(American Historical Association, Annual Report). Washington, D.C.:
Government Printing Office.

Du Bois, W.E.B. (1901). The Spawn of Slavery: The Convict Lease System in the South. Missionary Review of the World, 14, 737-745.

Dyson, Michael Eric. (2014). Berry Gordy talks black music with Michael Eric Dyson. The Grio: Entertainment. Retrieved from

http://thegrio.com/2014/06/30/berry-gordy-michael-eric-dyson-black-music/

Early, Gerald L. (2004). *One Nation Under a Groove : Motown and American Culture.* Ann Arbor, Michigan: University of Michigan Press.

Emery, Andrew. (1997). *Schoolly D- Original Gangsta.* Retrieved from www.globaldarkness.com/articles/schooly_d_original_gangsta.htm

Equiano, Olaudah. (2005). *The Interesting Narrative of the Life of Olaudah Equiano, Or Gustavus Vassa, The African.*

Fry, Gladys Marie. (1977). *Night Riders in Black Folk History.* Knoxville, Tennessee: University of Tennessee Press.

Gabbidon, S.L., & Greene, H.T. (2012). Race and Crime (3rd edition). Thousand Oaks, CA: Sage Publications.

Garber, Eric. (1983). *T'aint Nobody's Bizness, Homosexuality in 1920's Harlem,* in Black Men-White Men: Afro-American Gay Life and Culture. A Gay Anthology, ed. Michael J. Smith. San Francisco: Gay Sunshine Press.

Garber, Eric. (1989). *A Spectacle in Color: The Lesbian and Gay Subculture of Jazz Age Harlem.* Hidden from History. Eds. Martin Bauml Duberman, Martha Vicinus and George Chauncey Jr. New York: NAL Books, (p.318-331).

Garrow, David J. (1985). The Origins of the Montgomery Bus Boycott. *Journal of the Southern Regional Council* (Emory University) 7 (5): 24.

Gates, Henry Louis & Appiah, Anthony. (1999). *Africana: The Encyclopedia of the African and African American Experience.* Basic Civics Books. p.556.

Gilmore, Glenda Elizabeth. (2010) *Somewhere in the Nadir of African American History,*

   1890-1920. Freedom's Story, TeacherServe©. National Humanities Center.
   Retrieved from http://nationalhumanitiescenter.org/tserve/freedom/1865-
   1917/essays/nadir.htm

Gray, Thomas Ruffin (1831). *The Confessions of Nat Turner, the Leader of the Late
   Insurrections in Southampton, Va.* Baltimore, Maryland: Lucas & Deaver. pp.
   7–9, 11
Haley, Alex. (1965). *The Autobiography of Malcolm X: As Told To Alex Haley.* New York,

   New York: Grove Press.

Handler, M. S. (1964). Malcolm X Splits with Muhammad: Suspended Muslim Leader

   Plans Black Nationalist Political Movement. *New York Times.*

Hayslett, Chandra. (1996). Black Wallstreet Reveals Tragedy. The Daily Beacon.

   Retrieved from http://utdailybeacon.com/news/1996/feb/23/black-wallstreet-
   reveals-tragedy/.

Hutchinson, George. (2007). *The Cambridge Companion to the Harlem Renaissance.*

   New York: Cambridge University Press.

Johnson, A., & Johnson, R.(1979). *Propaganda and Aesthetics: The Literary Politics of*

   Afro-American Magazines in the Twentieth Century. Amherst: The University of

   Massachusetts Press, p.80-81.

Jones, Chenelle A. Dr. (July 25, 2012). The System Isn't Broken, It Was Designed That

   Way: A Critical Analysis of Historical Racial Disadvantage in the Criminal

   Justice System. Criminal Justice Analysis. Retrieved from

   http://www.hamptoninstitution.org/systemisntbroken.html#.VKSnJjOmerw

Jones & Modern Religious Utopias. AH: American History TV.

   Retrieved from http://series.c-span.org/Events/Lectures-in-History-Father-
   Divine-Jim-Jones-Modern-Religious-Utopias/10737443185-4/.

Kellner, Bruce. (1984). *The Harlem Renaissance: A Historical Dictionary for the Era.*

Westport, CN: Greenwood Press.

Klanwatch Project (2011). *Ku Klux Klan: a History of Racism and Violence* (Pamphlet)

(sixth edition). Montgomery, Alabama: Southern Poverty Law Center. p. 15.
Retrieved from
http://www.splcenter.org/sites/default/files/downloads/publication/Ku-Klux-Klan-
A-History-of-Racism.pdf.

Klein, Christopher. (2013). *10 Things You May Not Know About Martin Luther King Jr.*

History in the Headlines. Retrieved from http://www.history.com/news/10-
things-you-may-not-know-about-martin-luther-king-jr

Kneebone, John T. (2012). *Ku Klux Klan in Virginia.* Encyclopedia Virginia. Retrieved

from http://www.EncyclopediaVirginia.org/Ku_Klux_Klan_in_Virginia.

Koehlinger, Amy. (2013). *Lectures in History: Father Divine, Jim*

Lamb, Yvonne S. (2007). Irene M. Kirkaldy: Case Spurred Freedom Rides. *The*

Washington Post.

Lauterbach, Preston. (2011). *The Chitlin' Circuit: And the Road to Rock 'N' Roll.* New

York: W. W. Norton.

Lay, Shawn. (2005). Klu Klux Klan in the Twentieth Century. History & Archaeology:

Progressive Era to WWII, 1900-1945. New Georgia Encyclopedia. Retrieved
from http://www.georgiaencyclopedia.org/articles/history-archaeology/ku-klux-
klan-twentieth-century.

Levy, Peter B. (2011). The Dream Deferred: The Assassination of Martin Luther King, Jr.,

and the Holy Week Uprisings of 1968. in *Baltimore '68: Riots and Rebirth in an
American City.* By Jessica I. Elfenbein; Thomas L. Hollowak; Elizabeth M. Nix.
Philadelphia: Temple University Press.

Lieb, Sandra (1983). *Mother of the Blues: A Study of Ma Rainey* (3rd ed.). University of

Massachusetts Press.

Lott, Eric. (1995). *Love and Theft: Blackface Minstrelsy and The American Working*

    Class. Oxford University Press.

Lynch, Willie. (2009). *The Willie Lynch Letter and The Making of a Slave.* New York,

    New York: Classic Books America.

Madigan, Tim. (2001). *The Burning: Massacre, Destruction, and the Tulsa Race Riot of*

    1921. New York, New York: St Martin's Press, pp. 4, 131–132, 144, 159, 164,
    249.

Matthias, Blanche. (1923). Unknown Great Ones. The Woman Athletic.

Melton, John Gordan. (1965). *Father Divine: American religious*

    leader. Britannica Online Encyclopedia: Britannica.com. Retrieved from
    http://www.britannica.com/EBchecked/topic/166561/Father-Divine.

Mohn, Tanya. (2012). *Martin Luther King Jr.:*

    The German Connection and How He Got His Name. Forbes Online. Retrieved
    from http://www.forbes.com/sites/tanyamohn/2012/01/12/martin-luther-king-jr-
    the-german-connection-and-how-he-got-his-name/

Morrow, Alvin. (   ). Breaking the Curse of Willie Lynch: The

    Science of Slave Psychology. St. Louis, MO: Rising Sun Publications. (p.9).

Mosher, Donald L. and Serkin, M. (1984). Measuring a macho

    personality constellation. *Journal of Research in Personality*, 18 (2): 150-163.

Packard, Jerrold M. (2003). American Nightmare: The History of Jim Crow. New York,

    New York: St. Martin's Press, p.111.

Penrice, Ronda Racha. (2007). African American History for

    Dummies: Chapter 16: Give Me a Beat: African American Music. John Wiley &
    Songs, Inc. Hoboken, NJ. (p.309-315)

Perry, Bruce. (1989). Malcolm X: The Last Speeches. New York, New York: Pathfinder.

Reavis L. Mitchell Jr. (1995) Fisk University Since 1866: Thy Loyal Children Make Their

    Way. Retrieved from http://tennesseeencyclopedia.net/entry.php?rec=727)./

Rinehart, N.J. and McCabe, M.P. (1997). Hypersexuality: Psychopathology or normal

    variant of sexuality? *Sexual and Marital Therapy*, 45-60.

Ryan, Maureen. (2005). The Harlem Renaissance. *Scholastic Action* 28.9: 14.

    MasterFILE Premier. EBSCO. Web.

S.D., Trav. (2006). *No Applause-Just Throw Money: The Book That Made Vaudeville*

    Famous. New York: Faber & Faber Inc.

Salaam, Kaluma. (1997). Historical Overviews of The Black Arts Movement in *The*

    Oxford Companion to African American Literature. Oxford University Press.

Samuels, W. (2000). From the wild, wild west to Harlem's literary salons. *Black Issues*

    Book Review, 2(5), 14. Retrieved from Academic Search Elite database.

Scaruffi, Pierre. (2007). A history of Jazz Music 1900-2000. Chapter 4: New York Big

    Bands. Omniware: Self-Publishing. Retrieved from

    http://www.scaruffi.com/history/jazz4.html.

Smith, Jessie Carney. (2011). *Encyclopedia of African American Popular Culture*. Santa

    Barbara, California: Greenwood Press.

Sterling, Dorothy (1970). *Freedom Train: The Story of Harriet Tubman*. New York:
    Scholastic, Inc.
Stern, Carrie. (2012). *Savoy Ballroom*. Dance Heritage Coalition.

    Retrieved from http://www.danceheritage.org/treasures/savoy_essay_stern.pdf.

Strausbaugh, Jeremy P. (2006). *Black Like You: Blackface,*

    Whiteface, Insult & Imitation in American Popular Culture. Tarcher/Penguin
    Books.

Sweet, Frank W. (2000). A History of the Minstrel Show. Palm Coast, Florida:

    Backintyme.

Terres, John K. (1980). *Audubon Society Encyclopedia of North American Birds.* New
York: Knopf.

The Interactive Journal of Early American Life, Inc. (2001). *Common-Place.* Retrieved
from http://www.common-place.org/vol-01/no-04/school/elkins.shtml

Thompson, Gayle. (2014). *11 Years Ago: Natalie Maines Makes Controversial
Comments About President Bush.* Taste of Country Network. Retrieved from
http://theboot.com/natalie-maines-dixie-chicks-controversy/

Toll, Robert C. (1974). *Blacking Up: The Minstrel Show in Nineteenth-century America.*
New York: Oxford University Press.

Twain, Mark. (1917). *Autobiography of Mark Twain: The Complete and Authoritative
Edition, Vol.1.* New York, New York: HarperCollins.

Van Deburg, William L. (1992). *New Day in Babylon: The Black Power Movement and
American Culture, 1965-1975.* University of Chicago Press.

Vern E. Smith and Jon Meacham (1998). *Martin Luther King Jr.: The Legacy.*
Washington Post.

Watson, Steven. (1995). *The Harlem Renaissance.* New York: Pantheon Books.

Welsh, Kariamu. (2004). *African Dance.* Chelsea House Publishers, p. 19, 21. ISBN
0791076415

Whitaker, Matthew C. (2011). *Icons of Black America: Breaking Barriers and Crossing
Boundaries, Volume 1.* Santa Barbara, California: ABC-CLIO, LLC. (p.693).

Wiegand, Steve. (2014). U.S. History for Dummies (3rd edition): Slavery in America. John
Wiley & Songs, Inc. Hoboken, NJ.

Wintz, Cary D. and Finkelman, Paul, ed. (2004). *Encyclopedia of the Harlem
Renaissance (Vol. 2).* Taylor & Francis.

Young, Greg and Meyers, Tom. (May 2009). *The Bowery Boys*

> *New York City History: Jungle Alley and wild nights at Connie's Inn.* Retrieved
> from http://theboweryboys.blogspot.com/2009/05/jungle-alley-and-wild-nights-
> at-connies.html

Index

A

African drum, *28*
authentic
    authenticity, *101, 107, 285*

B

B.A.M
    Black Arts Movement, *283, 284, 285*
B.I.G., *12, 13*
Berry Gordy, *iii, 298, 299, 300, 302, 304, 307, 309, 311, 312, 315, 316, 321*
Black Panther Party, *iii, 281, 282, 286, 287, 289, 290, 291, 292, 293, 294, 295,*
    298
book smart, *135, 144, 145, 153, 154, 158, 214*
breakdancing, *v, 15, 20, 26, 39, 47, 97, 101, 114, 133, 158, 160, 178, 229, 241,*
    273, 279, 313

C

Civil Rights, *iii, 117, 235, 237, 238, 239, 240, 242, 243, 255, 258, 259, 260, 264,*
    266, 268, 271, 277, 279, 281, 282, 283, 298, 305, 310, 311, 312, 314, 319
clothing, *42, 82, 190, 259, 270, 280, 317*
common sense, *135, 145, 147, 153, 158, 215*

D

dj'ing
    Dj, *28, 81*
drugs, *91, 129, 162, 169, 186, 193, 231, 294, 308*
DuBois, *130, 134, 135, 137, 138, 139, 140, 141, 142, 143, 146, 149, 150, 151,*
    152, 153, 158, 159, 178, 221, 257

G

gangster, *82, 156, 158, 167, 170, 171, 172, 197, 215*
griot, *29, 30*

W